Praise for
Platform: Get Noticed in a Noisy World

"I've known Michael Hyatt for more than a decade, and during that time I've seen him master just about every social media platform that's hit the scene. He's used blogging, Facebook, Twitter, and more to expand his personal platform from a successful book publisher to a leading national brand of his own. Trust me, this guy knows what he's talking about—so pay attention!"

— **DAVE RAMSEY**
New York Times Best-selling Author
The Dave Ramsey Show

"A generous book from a man who knows what he's talking about. Michael Hyatt has built a platform, and you can too."

— **SETH GODIN**
New York Times Best-selling Author
of *We Are All Weird*

"Platform is absolutely essential to delivering value. As a big fan of Michael Hyatt, I'm excited he's sharing this with you. Your job? Learn about this and implement it. Your success depends on it."

— **CHRIS BROGAN**
President, Human Business Works
New York Times Best-selling Author

"Michael Hyatt is the authority on creating a platform in our crowded world, and *Platform* is the definitive, step-by-step guide to building a platform—from the ground up. If you're longing to become a true influencer in this world, Hyatt can teach you how. With *Platform*, Hyatt's done the near-impossible: create a guide even *more* useful than his wildly popular blog!"

— **CLAIRE DÍAZ ORTIZ**
Social Innovation
Twitter, Inc.

"I have watched Michael Hyatt build his own platform from the ground up to become one of the largest in the world. And he has done so with the strategies and tips he outlines in this very practical book. Any author, speaker, or small business owner who wants a blueprint for getting the attention and visibility they want, needs to read this book."

— **JOHN C. MAXWELL**
New York Times Best-selling Author
and Leadership Expert

"When I finished the last page of *Platform*, I realized I had more actionable notes from the book than from any other business book I've read in years. This is the definitive guidebook for building an online presence. Michael Hyatt, one of the pioneers of social networking and blogging, shares his successful blueprint for raising your visibility. Learn from his experience and save yourself time, money, and frustration by following his step-by-step advice."

— **SKIP PRICHARD**
President & CEO, Ingram Content
Group, Inc.

"In today's world, having an idea isn't enough to land a book or record deal, get a movie made, or find funding for your startup. You need a platform: A connected following that's ready to try, buy, and spread the word. Finally, in a single book, the blueprint for your platform is revealed by blog wunderkind Michael Hyatt. You'll finish this book slowly, because his simple but powerful advice will interrupt you with go-do-it-now urgency. Read it and expand your influence."

— **TIM SANDERS**
Former Chief Solutions Officer at
Yahoo
Author of *Today We Are Rich*

"For the last five years, if I ever had a question about platform building, social media, or standing out amidst the clutter, I turned to one place—Michael Hyatt. As an author who turned a blog into a book and made countless mistakes along the way, I couldn't get my hands on *Platform* fast enough. Michael Hyatt has written *THE* handbook to one of the biggest cultural revolutions in the last fifty years."

— **JON ACUFF**
Wall Street Journal Best-selling Author of *Quitter: Closing the Gap Between Your Day Job & Your Dream Job*

"Michael Hyatt offers step-by-step guidance on how to build a platform from the ground up. From starting a blog to creating an online media kit, from building a speaking page to getting more Twitter followers, it's all here—everything you need to know to build your own platform and start getting the attention you deserve."

— **ANDY ANDREWS**
New York Times Best-selling Author of *How Do You Kill 11 Million People, The Noticer,* and *The Traveler's Gift*

"I wish I had this book when I wrote my first book. Michael Hyatt has demystified what it takes to build and sustain a strong platform."

— **NANCY DUARTE**
Author of *Slideology* and *Resonate*
Principal, Duarte Design, Inc.

"Leaders are platform builders. And building a platform in today's noisy and distracted culture is tough, but Michael Hyatt understands what it takes to get there. Everything he writes about he has practiced and lived out. He has the know how and influence that you'll want to learn from, providing expertise on the who and what for platform building. This book is important, timely, and deeply practical for any leader hoping to expand their reach and influence, and raise the visibility of their brand, product, service, or cause. I highly recommend it!"

— **BRAD LOMENICK**
President, Catalyst

"Michael Hyatt has put together the most comprehensive and easy-to-follow resource on platform-building I've seen. Not only is his method dead-on accurate and trustworthy, it's also DO-able, because he's actually done it and proven that it works. I'd recommend his advice to all authors, and as a businessperson, I'm following it too."

— **RACHELLE GARDNER**
Literary Agent, Books & Such

"Yes, talent, desire, and passion are key elements for success as an author, musician, artist, coach, or speaker. But this book identifies the elephant in the room—the other 90 percent of the process necessary to have a voice in today's arena."

— **DAN MILLER**
Creative Thinker at 48Days.net
and Author of *48 Days to the Work You Love*

"Michael Hyatt is a pioneer in social media who is now generously sharing his 'secrets' with those of us who have been marveling at his success for many years. Whether you are a seasoned writer, blogger, speaker, and social media enthusiast, or just now starting out, this book will help you take that next step and begin to build a platform of your own."

— **DAN T. CATHY**
President & COO, Chick-fil-A, Inc.

"Michael Hyatt is a master of clear communication with major takeaway. He has a gift for conquering complex problems with doable steps and memorable strategies. This book is a must-read for anyone hoping to bring awareness to their product, service, or mission."

— **CRAIG GROESCHEL**
Senior Pastor of LifeChurch.tv
Author of *Soul Detox, Clean Living in a Contaminated World*

"Masterful communicators walk their talk. Michael Hyatt is masterful. The congruency between what he says and how he lives rings true, so lean in and learn. He crams life into every sentence, so get ready to experience an explosion of ideas!"

— **PATSY CLAIRMONT**
Author of *Stained Glass Hearts*

"For business owners, speakers, authors, or anyone who is adamant that they have a message to share, this is the book for you. Michael has nailed it from concept to creation to connection. If you want to be heard, there have to be ears pointing in your direction! *Platform* is the perfect formula for getting as many ears as possible in listening range so you can be heard above the rest of the clamor."

— **CARRIE WILKERSON**
Author of *The Barefoot Executive*
Host of BarefootExecutive.TV

"Finally! A book that goes beyond the usual fluff you hear and tells you how to actually build an audience. Michael Hyatt's *Platform* is the essential guide to finding your true fans and keeping them. I am recommending this book to every author, artist, and entrepreneur I know—and probably will be for years."

— **JEFF GOINS**
Author of *Wrecked: When a Painful World Slams into Your Comfortable Life*

"*Platform* is a book you can open to any chapter and find a list of practical actions you can put on your calendar today that will begin building your platform immediately. This information is crucial for anyone trying to capture the eyes, ears, and hearts of people in today's world. I am purchasing a copy for my entire team, so we can go through it together and implement this strategy."

— **KEN DAVIS**
Author of *Fully Alive*
Speaker and Communications Trainer

"This isn't just a book, it's a flatbed truck full of construction materials which just backed up to your door. Michael Hyatt doesn't just give us a pile of wood, a bag of concrete, some nails and tell us to start building. He gives us a set of plans that have worked for him and he gives us practical and insightful ideas in this book about how we can build some scaffolding around our dreams."

— **BOB GOFF**
Author of *Love Does: Discover a Secretly Incredible Life in an Ordinary World*

"I've watched Michael Hyatt successfully build his platform over the past few years. As a result, I've learned a ton about the importance of building a platform, engaging the tribe, and adding value to the conversation. His ability to inspire WOW pushes me to continually change my online strategy and improve. I can't wait for you to read this book. It will be everything you need to build your platform and make a difference in the world—even starting from zero."

— **SPENCE SMITH**
Artist Relations Director, USA
Compassion International

"So you have a message that needs to be heard, but you lack the 'know how' or dollars required to get your message out. In other words, you don't have a *platform*. My friend and client Michael Hyatt will change that for you. Buy this book, read it, and apply it. Get your message out to all of us who need to hear it. He can and will help you."

— **DANIEL HARKAVY**
CEO & Executive Coach, Building Champions, Inc.

"Michael Hyatt is my first source at learning how to build my own platform. Everything he writes, I read. Everything he does, I try to emulate in some form, because I know when he writes it, is coming from personal experience and success. In a day when everyone needs a platform to succeed, this is a needed book."

— **RON EDMONDSON**
Pastor, Grace Community Church
Leadership Blogger at RonEdmondson.com

"Michael Hyatt has given much of his professional career to helping others achieve their potential. And he helps others by pioneering a way and then teaching people his way. In Platform, he's accumulated the best of his counsel and advice. If you'd like to expand your influence, read Platform and then read it again."

— **DONALD MILLER**
New York Times Bestselling Author of *A Million MIles in a Thousand Years*

"Michael Hyatt's *Platform* is exactly what every entrepreneur and forward-thinker needs to build an effective, winsome platform—the kind that woos tribe members and inspires action. Hyatt demystifies social media through friendly step-by-step instructions, interesting stories, and hard facts. Not only does he inspire you to look at platform differently, he emulates what he writes."

— **MARY DEMUTH**
Author of 14 books

"Michael Hyatt is one of my heroes. I follow his lead on almost everything. My business and personal life have been radically transformed by his example. Over the years I have learned that one of the shortcuts to success is the concept of modeling. If you want to be successful with your "Platform" then study what Mike has learned and applied in his new book. Otherwise, you'll probably end up as one of the casualties we see all too often in the industry."

— **MIKE SMITH**
President/CEO
Michael Smith & Associates
Veteran Artist Manager

"Mike Hyatt is a platform Guru who created an international following that went from nothing to WOW in record time. In this amazing book Platform he reveals his success secrets taking the reader from WOW to HOW. Anyone wanting to succeed at marketing a product such as themselves will find Platform an invaluable handbook for success."

— **STEVE ARTERBURN**
Best-selling author, founder of
Women of Faith
Host of Newlife Live radio and
television talk show

PLATFORM

GET NOTICED IN A NOISY WORLD

MICHAEL HYATT

THOMAS NELSON
Since 1798

NASHVILLE DALLAS MEXICO CITY RIO DE JANEIRO

To all the authors, artists, and creatives I've met through the years who have been turned away because they didn't have a platform. This book is for you.

Published in Nashville, Tennessee, by Thomas Nelson. Thomas Nelson is a registered trademark of Thomas Nelson, Inc.

Page design by Walter Petrie.

Thomas Nelson, Inc., titles may be purchased in bulk for educational, business, fund-raising, or sales promotional use. For information, please e-mail SpecialMarkets@ThomasNelson.com.

Unless otherwise noted, Scripture quotations are taken from the King James Version.

Library of Congress Cataloging-in-Publication Data

Hyatt, Michael S.
Platform : get noticed in a noisy world / Michael Hyatt.
p. cm.
Includes bibliographical references and index.
ISBN 978-1-59555-503-8
1. Social networks. 2. Success in business. 3. Success. I. Title.
HM741.H935 2012
302.3—dc23 2012006063

Printed in the United States of America

12 13 14 15 16 QGF 6 5 4 3 2 1

Contents

Part Three: Build Your Home Base

Part Four: Expand Your Reach

INTRODUCTION

All the World's a Stage

More than four centuries ago, William Shakespeare wrote, "All the world's a stage," and his words are truer today than ever before. If you have something to say—through a blog, a seminar, a book, a song, a screenplay, a sermon, or a stage play—you are on stage. If you have something to sell—whether one-on-one, before a huge crowd, or on the Internet—you are also on stage.

But the stage has never been more crowded—and simply being on it doesn't matter much if the lights are not shining on you, or if there is no one in the audience.

This book is all about attracting that audience, turning on the brightest lights you can find, and building passionate loyalty so your audience stays with you through every line, every scene, every act. It's not about ego or being the center of attention. It is about having something of value to others and finding the most powerful way of getting that message to others who can benefit from it.

If you are an aspiring (or already successful) author, artist, musician, public speaker, salesperson, candidate for public office—anyone who has something to say or sell—I want to help you take the stage and get noticed beyond your wildest imagination.

THE NEW STAGE

You've likely never heard of me prior to picking up this book, unless you are somehow connected with publishing or you follow my blog. After all,

I'm not a celebrity, and I don't have a talk show on cable TV, nor have I recorded a number one Billboard hit, or run for—or held—public office. (Thank goodness.)

Yet despite all that, I already have something you need—something you should deeply desire, if you want to achieve success in your field. It's called a *platform*.

Very simply, a platform is the thing you have to stand on to get heard. It's your stage. But unlike a stage in the theater, today's platform is not built of wood or concrete or perched on a grassy hill. Today's platform is built of people. Contacts. Connections. Followers.

Your platform is the means by which you connect with your existing and potential fans. It might include your company website, a blog, your Twitter and Facebook accounts, an online video show, or a podcast. It may also include your personal appearances as a public speaker, musician, or entertainer. It might even include traditional media such as a newspaper column, magazine articles, or radio show. It most likely will include a combination of all these items.

THE WHO

As in times past, success today is not so much about *what* you know; it's about *who* you know. And the *who* is your platform. You may already have—or believe you have—a significant *what*. But you have to make yourself heard amidst the noise of thousands of other voices; you also have to be able to present your brilliant, significant what to someone. I can help you find and connect with the who in the equation.

You may wonder why you should listen to me on this subject. Here's why. My blog, MichaelHyatt.com, has more than four hundred thousand monthly visitors. In addition, more than fifty thousand people subscribe to my daily blog posts. In fact, this book is based, in large part, on many of my posts on social networking. So many people requested that I put all my thoughts on the subject down in one place that I finally sat down and did just that (with some significant additions). I also have more than one hundred thousand Twitter followers and fifteen thousand Facebook fans.

And that has all happened in the last eight years.

As a person who has connected with a lot of whos, I can tell you with certainty that building a platform is no longer about being picked by a gatekeeper; investing thousands of dollars in consultants; or understanding complex and confusing technology.

This may have been the reality five years ago. But not today. Social media technologies have changed everything. Now, for the first time in history, noncelebrities—people like you and me—can get noticed and win big in an increasingly noisy world.

THE EQUATION

I received an e-mail message a few days ago from an aspiring author trying to make a name for herself amidst her literally millions of competitors. The book-publishing world is one of the noisiest. This is a perfect example of someone who believes her book (the what) should be sufficient for success. Her message was typical of what I hear on a weekly basis as the chairman of the board of Thomas Nelson Publishers. She wrote,

> Two respected agents have told me they loved my book and proposal and are willing to represent it, but not until I have social media followers numbering in the thousands. I find this bewildering: Doesn't a good book stand on its own anymore? Are writers now doomed to spend the bulk of our workdays trawling for blog subscribers?

The answer to the first question is no. A good product does not stand on its own anymore. It is foundational, but it is not enough. The answer to the second question is yes. You will need to be proactive about creating the who part of the equation. In order for you to be successful in today's business environment, you need two things: a compelling product *and* a significant platform.

It is just not sufficient to build a cool product, craft a compelling message, compose a beautiful piece of music, write a scintillating novel, or champion an important cause. This is true now more than ever. Why? Two reasons:

1. **Competition has never been greater.** Have you shopped online recently? I was looking at flat-screen TVs on Amazon the other day, and there were 19,069 results from my search! That's ludicrous, but it's the reality you are facing if you're trying to get your message across about something you're trying to sell.
2. **People are more distracted than ever.** It's not just that we have more products available. We have more of every kind of media available. More movies. More television channels. More apps, radio stations, podcasts, and video games. More news sites, blogs, and, of course, Facebook and Twitter. In other words, people's attention is a *finite resource*, and you're in competition against every other media that wants a slice of your prospective customer's attention.

This can be discouraging, as it was to the aspiring author who contacted me, but I choose to see it as an opportunity. Never before have there been so many ways you can connect with people if you do it right. That's where building a platform comes in.

There are at least three benefits to carefully building and nurturing your platform:

1. **A platform provides visibility.** The word *platform* itself is a metaphor for the stage I talked about earlier—a stage on which you are elevated above the crowd. It makes it possible for everyone in the audience to see you. This is especially important in our noisy world, where more and more people and organizations are screaming for our attention.
2. **A platform provides amplification.** It enables you to be heard above the roar of the crowd. The noise. Long before modern sound systems, preachers and politicians stood on platforms in order to be heard. Modern sound systems leverage natural acoustics and make it possible to speak before tens of thousands of people. Today, modern media—especially social media—provide an opportunity for you to extend your reach even further.
3. **A platform provides connection.** Traditional media platforms make possible a kind of unilateral intimacy. You "know" the talk show

host, the performing artist, or the conference speaker. But social media has taken this to a whole new level. It makes possible bilateral intimacy—*engagement*. The result is that you can be more connected to your fans, customers, and supporters than ever before.

Now that you understand the basic concept of platform, here's how I'll guide you through the construction of a solid, enduring stage for you, your products, your services, or your cause.

In *Platform*'s first section, Start with Wow, you will discover how to create, name, and package a compelling product (the what). If you don't have that right, nothing else matters. Once you have that nailed down, you can dive into the who.

The Prepare to Launch section covers everything from setting up your branding tools to securing raving endorsements and creating an online media kit.

Then move on to the Build Your Home Base section (where we get into the nitty-gritty of building a powerful website home for yourself) and Expand Your Reach, which covers blogging, Twitter, and Facebook. Finally we'll wrap it up in Engage Your Tribe, with some valuable information about monitoring your brand and engaging with your audience.

Platform is designed to be as user-friendly as possible. You may want to read the whole thing in order, or you can find a topic that interests you and dive right in. Each chapter stands alone. (I have no doubt many of you will jump right to the last chapter, "Monetize Your Blog.") You will find an index at the end for detailed searches.

PART ONE

START WITH WOW

ONE

Create a Compelling Product

Now you know there are two critical parts of the success equation: a compelling product (the what) and a significant platform (the who). In this book you will find a wealth of information on the second element in the equation, but if you don't slam-dunk the first element—the compelling product—you won't win the game.

There is no sense in wasting your valuable time and resources trying to build a buzz about a ho-hum product. As one of my favorite marketing gurus, David Ogilvy, once wrote, "Great marketing only makes a bad product fail faster." How true.

For years I have argued, "It's the product, stupid." The secret to success in any business is to deliver a great, compelling product. And when I say *product*, I mean anything you are trying to say or sell. It may be yourself, if you're a speaker or entertainer. It might be a stellar service you provide for profit or nonprofit. Perhaps it's a cause you are championing, a message you are passionate about. Or it could be an actual physical product, like a book. Regardless of the form your product takes, no amount of marketing savvy, salesmanship, or operational excellence can overcome a weak product.

The purpose of marketing is to prime the pump. But if people don't want to use your product and—more importantly—if they won't recommend it to their friends, you're hosed. You can't spend enough money or be clever enough to overcome a lack of word-of-mouth marketing. It just won't work.

In light of this, it was fascinating to watch how Apple first introduced the iPhone. Like millions of other Mac fans, I read all the articles and even worked my way through Apple's slick, interactive website. I thought to myself, *Very cool. I definitely want one of these.* But I also thought, *I can wait until the second generation. Let them work out the bugs first.*

But then I watched Steve Job's 2007 keynote presentation from MacWorld. If you are involved in any aspect of product development, this is a must-watch video.[1]

I garnered three insights:

1. **Create products you would personally use.** Watching Steve, you get the sense he loves the product. He is so familiar with it, because he has been using it. He thinks it is "way cool," and he's not afraid to say so. He sprinkles words like *awesome*, *incredible*, and even *magical* throughout his speech. He exhibits the wonder of a five-year-old on Christmas morning. You really believe him. He's not trying to sell you something. He's simply sharing the experience.

   What about the products you create? If you're speaking about business, do you deliver exciting and powerful messages that you know can make a difference in people's lives? If you're in sales, do you even use the items you sell? Would you recommend them enthusiastically to a friend? Do you really love these products or are you only trying to meet some arbitrary quota or generate revenue?

2. **Create products that solve problems in unexpected ways.** It was interesting to watch some of the biggest cell phone manufacturers get hammered in the press the week before the iPhone was announced. They essentially said, "We've saturated the market. There's nothing compelling left to build. Investors need to get used to the idea of slower revenue growth and tighter margins. From this point forward, competition is going to be brutal."

   Then Steve announced a new phone that essentially reinvented the category. Not surprisingly, Apple's stock soared. Motorola's, Nokia's, and Samsung's took a nosedive.

   Apple wasn't content to create a phone that just had additional features. It completely rethought the solution—from the ground up.

Apple's engineers put themselves in the user's place and refused to be constrained by the past. They didn't start with the technology. They started with the dream and then went in search of technology. This is a completely different way of doing business.

What about you? We too often think *inside* the box. We let the past constrain us. We don't get in the consumers' shoes and ask, "What would make this really cool? What would take this to a whole new level? What would we create if the limits of current technology weren't an issue?" You have to get outside the box and learn to dream again.

3. **Create products that exceed your customers' expectations.** As I watched Steve's presentation, I couldn't help but notice the crowd. It was like they were watching a master magician. As Steve demonstrated each new feature, the crowd erupted in applause. To my surprise, I found myself laughing with glee. I felt like a kid again. Most of all, I wanted one of those phones!

   Part of the charm is that Apple seems to execute its product vision with such amazing simplicity and elegance. Every icon on the phone is understated but beautiful. Every feature is easy to use but not complex. Everything seems not only as good as Apple could make it but as good as Apple could *imagine* it.

   What about your products or services? How often have you rushed something to market with a sigh and a collective, "Well, I guess that will have to do. It's not great, but it's good enough"?

   Sadly, we don't start with a lofty vision. I'm afraid we have become content with mediocrity; we aim low and execute even lower.

If you want to build a platform, it's time to get the passion back. Push one another and yourself to deliver great products that you are delighted—yes, delighted!—to offer. If you don't, then your attempt to build a platform is doomed to failure.

If you create outstanding products, everything else becomes much easier. Apple spends a fortune on product development. But relatively speaking, it doesn't spend much on marketing. Nevertheless, when it introduced the iPhone, Apple got more press coverage than the entire

Consumer Electronics Show that was going on simultaneously in Las Vegas. Apple has proven beyond a shadow of a doubt that "it's the product, stupid."

Let's take a lesson from the Apple playbook and get the first part of the success equation right: start with a wow product.

TWO

Bake in the Wow

Now I want to tell you about Blake Mycoskie, who creates wows of a different, but no less magical, kind than the late Steve Jobs.

In 2006, Mycoskie was traveling in Argentina and saw that many children there had no shoes. So when he returned home to America, he created a new company, TOMS Shoes. For every pair sold, TOMS matches it—one for one—with a pair of new shoes given to a child in need. When he returned to Argentina with reinforcements the next year, they placed ten thousand pairs on little feet. And by September 2010, TOMS and its affiliated partners such as Feed The Children had given more than one million pairs to kids in need around the world.[1]

Now, you may not think a pair of shoes is a wow product, but for many of these kids, TOMS shoes will be their very first pair. Without shoes they cannot go to school, and they are susceptible to soil-transmitted diseases that penetrate the skin. One child in Kenya said, "I'm excited because when I woke up in the morning, I did not know when I'll have something like this." And a teacher said, "I can tell you, these children will not sleep today. They will be talking about those shoes the whole night!"[2] Now that's *wow*.

If you, like Steve Jobs or Blake Mycoskie, have a message to share, or a product or service to sell, I have significant news for you. We don't need more messages or products or services. Instead, we need *better* messages, products, and services. Specifically, we need those that wow. This is the "compelling product" part of the success equation. But what is wow and how can we develop it? How can we make sure our message, product, or service creates a wow experience?

The first step is learning to recognize it. Most of us have experienced wow moments. We just haven't taken time to think deeply about them.

For example, a few summers ago, I took my wife and youngest daughter to Scotland. It was our first visit. We rented a car and spent a week touring the western Highlands. We started in Edinburgh and drove north to Inverness. We then drove down the west side of Loch Ness to Fort Augusta and then headed west across the Highlands to the Isle of Skye. We took our time and savored every moment.

As we neared the town of Portree, the capital of Skye, we saw the Sound of Raasay for the first time and let out a collective, "Wow!" It was gorgeous. My eyes welled up with tears. It was a transcendent moment—something none of us had expected.

We experienced numerous wow moments on this trip—Edinburgh Castle, the Caledonian Canal, Eilean Donan Castle, the ancient Dun Telve Broch, Glenelg Bay, Kilt Rock, the church of St. Mary and St. Finnan near Glenfinnan, and the endless fields of Scottish lupines.

Sometime after that trip, I met with my executive team for an all-day planning meeting. As we began the afternoon session, I asked them to think of one of the most powerful wow moments they had experienced in their lives. Then I asked each person to share the experience. One person spoke about the birth of a child. Another told of the first time he kissed his wife. Still another shared his experience of seeing Victoria Falls in Zimbabwe for the first time. It was so inspiring. We all could see each person's face light up as he or she spoke. The rest of us vicariously entered into the joy.

Next I asked the group to try to identify the common attributes in each of these experiences. Here's the list we created. Every wow experience has some combination of the following ten elements:

1. **Surprise**. A wow experience always exceeds our expectations. It creates delight, amazement, wonder, or awe. For Christmas one year, one of my friends bought me a copy of the illustrated edition of *1776* by David McCullough.[3] Honestly, it blew my socks off. I have never seen a more beautiful book. As the advertising copy says, "Packed with striking replicas of letters, maps, and portraits, this updated

version of David McCullough's 2005 best seller provides readers with unedited firsthand accounts of America's initial steps toward sovereignty." This product definitely created a wow experience.

2. **Anticipation**. Anticipating a wow experience is almost as good as the experience itself. As you think about it, you begin to live it in advance. For example, as I am writing this, Gail and I are planning a trip to the beach. We are beginning to think about it daily. I am making a mental list of the things I want to do. I can almost feel the breeze blowing in from the ocean. With each new day, the anticipation builds.
3. **Resonance**. A wow experience touches the heart. It resonates at a deep level. It sometimes causes goose bumps or even tears. I remember watching my two granddaughters play on the beach for the first time. They were joy personified as they chased the waves and the waves chased them. I thought to myself, *Oh, to be that young!*
4. **Transcendence**. A wow experience connects you to something transcendent. In that moment, you experience purpose, meaning, or even God. Years ago when I was an artist manager, one of my clients sat down at a piano to play some new songs for my business partner and me. As she began to sing, I was caught up in the music. I knew her talent was coming directly from some other place. I was overwhelmed at the beauty.
5. **Clarity**. A wow experience creates a moment when you see things with more clarity than ever before. You suddenly "get it" in a new way. Not long ago, I was reading *Chasing Daylight* by Eugene O'Kelly.[4] The story was so powerful I could not put it down. I read it in one long airplane ride to the West Coast. In those few hours, I had more clarity about life than I had had in a long time.
6. **Presence**. A wow experience creates timelessness. You aren't thinking about the past. You're not even thinking about the future. Instead, you are fully present in what is happening now. One such perfect moment happened when I enjoyed an evening on the porch with my daughter, Mary, and her husband, Chris. We spent several hours talking and enjoying a bottle of wine together. It seemed like time stood still.

7. **Universality**. A true wow experience is nearly universal. Almost everyone will experience it in a similar way. This is why Cirque du Soleil and the Grand Canyon are so popular. They are so compelling that they appeal to people of all ages and ethnicities.
8. **Evangelism**. A wow experience has to be shared. You can't contain it. You immediately begin thinking of all the people you wish were with you. After the experience, you recommend it unconditionally. You become an unpaid evangelist. I have done this with all the books I recommend to my friends and on my blog. And as you might know, "Apple evangelists" are a phenomenon of their own.
9. **Longevity**. The shine never wears off a wow experience. You can experience it again and again without growing tired of it. It endures. In 1973 I attended a Crosby, Stills, Nash & Young concert at Texas Stadium in Dallas, Texas. I was on the field, about ten yards from the stage. It was incredible. In 2000, for my birthday, Gail bought tickets to the CSN&Y concert in Nashville. Twenty-seven years later, they still blew me away.
10. **Privilege**. A wow experience makes you proud in a good way. You're glad to be associated with it. You feel privileged, as if you are in an elite group, but at the same time humbled that you have had the experience. "Sandra" had a wow experience following her cochlear implant surgery. She had become profoundly deaf by the time she had the implants. On Activation Day, she was able to hear her granddaughter's first words to her: "Can you hear me, Grandma?" Within months her hearing was clear, and "the magic began. I heard grandchildren's voices for the first time, and my children, family and friends sounded just as I remembered. Does life get any better than this?"[5] Clearly Sandra feels both privileged and humbled.

Being successful means becoming the expert in recognizing wow when it shows up. More importantly, it means being able to recognize it when it is absent—and insisting that you ask yourself to deliver it. Don't settle for something less, because, in doing so, you are depriving your customers of the wow experience they seek—and deserve. It is the foundation to building a significant platform.

THREE

Exceed Market Expectations

On November 28, 2010, the highly anticipated Broadway rock musical *Spider-Man: Turn Off the Dark* had its preview showing. Audiences were excited to see the sold-out show, since it was directed by Julie Taymor, who had also directed the spectacular musical adaptation of *The Lion King*. And the score would be outstanding too; the music and lyrics were written by Bono and the Edge, half of U2. At a cost of sixty-five million dollars, the production was to be one of visually stunning special effects.

It was, however, an utter disaster. The four-hour mess started late, had a hopelessly muddled plot, and was "stopped repeatedly as equipment fell from the rafters and actors were left hanging in the air."[1]

The lead actor, Reeve Carney, was "caught in an aerial harness at one point, while also being dangled several feet in the air above the audience at the end of act one."[2]

Of the eighteen hundred or so people in the audience that night, some walked out. Here are some of their comments:[3]

- "OK, I have no idea what I just witnessed. It was a total incoherent mess. Taymor seems to have gotten so caught up in the symbolism and fx that she forgot to include a story. Innovative at times, but soulless always."
- "The show was stopped 5–6 times. During one of those times in the second act, a woman in the audience screamed out . . . 'I don't know about anybody else, but I feel like a guinea pig and I want my money back!' We should all get refunds."

- "Oh. Plot. Right. . . . Act I was understandable. Act II was bizarre. It was completely lost. The show is meant to be meaningful, I guess?"

Spider-Man's audience that night was expecting a wow experience, and what Taymor delivered was, to put it mildly, disappointing. That is something we all wish to avoid, even if on a smaller and less public scale.

Here's the bottom line: *you must exceed the customer's current expectations.*

That doesn't sound all that profound. But I think it has big implications for those of us who are committed to creating wow experiences—and building significant platforms.

First of all, each person brings a specific set of expectations to each experience. Those expectations may be conscious or unconscious. They may be general or specific. They may be vague or clearly defined. Regardless, no customer comes to any experience without some kind of expectation. It's just the way the human mind works.

In the case of *Spider-Man: Turn Off the Dark*, several things shaped audience expectations: their previous experience with the very popular *Spider-Man* movies; the reputations of the director, Julie Taymor (famous from *The Lion King*), and the score writer, musical icon Bono; their familiarity with the character on which the musical was based; and the commercials and ads they had seen.

The point is that each one came to the musical with a very defined set of expectations. Note also the use of the word *current* in my definition above. Our expectations for staged plays were different twenty years ago; we didn't have such things as CG and computer-aided lighting for special effects. Each successive wow creates a new threshold for the next one.

In any event, *Spider-Man*'s audience members could have had three different experiences relative to their expectations:

- Disappointing: the experience did not meet their expectations
- Good: the experience met their expectations
- Wow: the experience exceeded their expectations

Please note that only the last one is a wow experience. The other two are *not*-wow. Good is not good enough. If you are committed to creating a wow experience, then only the last of these three experiences is an acceptable outcome.

By the way, you don't have to make every experience in life a wow. If everything is a wow, then pretty soon, nothing is a wow. But you must be able to identify which experiences you want to make a wow, and then have a process—or a technology—for creating that outcome. I call this "the how of wow." The answers to these five questions will help you determine if your product is compelling:

1. What is the product or experience I want to create or transform into a wow?
2. How will the customer or prospect feel as a result of this experience? (In other words, what is the specific outcome you want to create?)
3. What specific expectations does the typical customer bring to this experience?
4. What does failing to meet customers' expectations for this experience look like?
5. What does exceeding customers' expectations for this experience look like?

These questions can be used on your own or in a group setting to create a wow conversation.

To illustrate, let's say that we have realized our product is more than the thing we produce. It is the total customer experience, and it begins from the moment our customers walk into our corporate lobby. We determine that we want to make this a wow experience. Here's one way we could apply the questions:

1. What is the product or experience I want to create or transform into a wow? The customer's lobby experience.
2. How will the customer feel as a result of this experience? (In other words, what is the specific outcome we want to create?) The customer

should feel we must be an extraordinary company because he has never had a lobby experience like this. He assumes we are somehow really different, and can't wait to experience more.

3. What specific expectations does the typical customer bring to this experience?

- The lobby should be clean, neat, and well lit.
- The receptionist should be friendly and professional.
- The receptionist will call the appropriate person and notify him he has a visitor.
- He will be asked to sign in and put on a visitor's name badge.
- He will be seated while he waits.
- He'll wait five to ten minutes before being admitted.
- There will be a few, probably slightly out-of-date magazines to thumb through.
- The person he's here to see will meet him in the lobby.

4. What does failing to meet customers' expectations for this experience look like?

- The lobby is dirty, messy, or dimly lit.
- The receptionist is distracted, cold, or rude.
- The receptionist interrogates the customer, almost as if she is asking him to prove he has an appointment.
- He is told (not asked) to sign in and handed a cheap, adhesive label on which to print his name. The label keeps falling off his coat.
- There is nowhere to sit or all the seats are occupied. He must stand.
- He has to wait more than ten minutes.
- There is either nothing to read or the magazines are badly worn and outdated.
- He is told where to go and has to navigate a building he has never been in.

5. What does exceeding customers' expectations for this experience look like?

- The lobby is clean, neat, well lit, and beautiful. It is decorated with interesting artifacts from the company's history with little cards explaining the significance of each one. A running fountain and a small indoor pond create a soothing oasis from the noise of the street outside.
- The receptionist's title is Director of First Impressions. She understands the strategic importance of her job and takes great pride in her role at the company.
- The receptionist always refers to visitors as *guests*. The term *visitor* implies someone who doesn't quite belong and whom everyone hopes leaves quickly. The term *guest* implies someone who is to be honored and shown hospitality.
- The receptionist warmly greets the guest by name. The guest wonders, *How did she know that?* The receptionist extends her hand and introduces herself. She says, "It is so nice to meet you [or see you again]. We're glad you've come by today!" or "It's so nice to see you again. The weather is a lot warmer than when you were here in March."
- She then hands him a preprinted guest badge. (If the guest came in unannounced, she quickly prints a badge.) It is magnetic, rather than adhesive or a pin. It sticks to his jacket without damaging the fabric. The guest's first name is in large letters; his last name is printed in smaller letters underneath it.
- The receptionist asks the guest if he'd care for something to drink. "I have bottled water, soda, or freshly brewed Starbucks coffee," she says. If the guest says, "Coffee," the receptionist asks how the guest likes it.
- The receptionist then says, "If you would like to have a seat, I will call [name] and tell him you are here. I know he's looking forward to seeing you. While we're waiting for him to come down, I'll get your coffee."
- The guest sits down on a comfortable chair and notices a selection of the most recent edition of several popular magazines, as

well as a few industry journals. In addition, there is a stack of one of our new products. A small card next to the stack invites guests to take a copy with our compliments.

- The receptionist signs the guest in herself, after the guest is seated. This process is completely invisible to the guest.
- Within five minutes, the person with whom the guest has an appointment steps into the lobby and warmly greets the guest. As they leave the lobby, the receptionist says, "It was good to meet you, [name]. I look forward to seeing you later."

This is, of course, just an example. But I think it illustrates how you can transform any experience (even an ordinary one) into a wow experience. This process can really be applied to anything—a family vacation, a date with your spouse, a company meeting, or, yes, even the creation of a new product.

The challenge, of course, is in the execution. How do you make your vision of wow become a reality? This is what separates the great products from the merely good. It is also what sets you up to build a powerful platform.

As I said previously, you don't have to make everything a wow. But once you learn the distinction between wow and *not*-wow, it is difficult to be satisfied with anything less.

FOUR

Beware of the Obstacles

Some time ago, while I was still the CEO of Thomas Nelson Publishers, I had an interesting conversation with one of our editors. He had just finished reading a new manuscript from one of our biggest authors. I asked, "So what did you think?"

He hesitated. "Honestly?"

"Yes. I want the truth," I assured him.

"Not great."

My heart sank. I knew we had invested a great deal of money in this book and were counting on significant sales from it.

"Okay . . . so what's wrong with it?" I asked, not knowing if I really wanted the truth.

"I . . . I don't know," he stammered. "It just feels like the same-old-same-old. I didn't really see anything new here that he hasn't said before."

"That's a problem," I said, stating the obvious. "This project is too important to settle for anything less than wow."

You, too, have a choice in the projects and dreams you pursue. You can hold out for wow, or you can settle for something less.

In my experience, there are at least five obstacles to creating wow experiences:

1. **We simply run out of time.** The deadline looms. We are scrambling to get the product out the door. Or we have to wrap up the service so we can get to the next client before he starts complaining. We simply

don't have the time to give the job our best effort, so we let it go. Half-baked. Before it is really done.

2. **We don't have enough resources.** We'd like to do a better job. We sincerely want to take it to the next level. But we just don't have the money or the staffing. We rationalize by saying, "I did the best I could do with the resources I had." And again, we let it go and turn our attention to the next project or client in the queue.
3. **We don't have sufficient experience.** We just don't know how to do what we know needs to be done. Our vision exceeds our know-how. We know what the product or service could deliver, but we don't have the knowledge, the skills, or the experience to get us there. So we settle for something less than our vision demands.
4. **Too often, we acquiesce to the committee.** Perhaps we are a little unsure of ourselves. "Everyone else seems to like it," we say to ourselves. "Maybe they're right. There are a lot of smart people in this room. C'mon, just let it go!" And so we do. We dial back our own vision for what could be and succumb to the collective judgment of the group.
5. **But the biggest obstacle of all is fear.** In fact, this is the primary obstacle. If we are honest, we must admit that the previous four items are only excuses. If we had enough courage, we would find the time, the resources, or the experience. We would stand up to the committee. We wouldn't settle for something less than wow.

But what are we really afraid of? Perhaps we fear losing our job, our client, or our influence. Maybe we don't want to be thought of as unreasonable or demanding. We are afraid of what others might say behind our back. Instead, we want to be liked.

If we are going to create wow experiences, we must become courageous. This is a personal, psychological bridge we need to cross. What we want to create—that wow experience—is on the other side of the ravine. There's no other way to get there from here.

FIVE

Don't Settle for Less than Great

Five years after we were married, Gail and I went to Maui to celebrate our anniversary. On the second day, we took snorkeling lessons. We started in the swimming pool, then progressed to the coral reef next to our hotel. We loved it. It was like swimming in a huge aquarium.

Later that same day, we rented some snorkeling gear and determined that we would venture out on our own. We had discovered a new sport that we could do together.

The next morning we ventured down to the beach. There wasn't another soul around. It was like a scene from *Blue Lagoon*—pristine, tranquil, and stunning. We couldn't wait to get into the water.

As we paddled about in the lagoon, facing down in the water, we were mesmerized by the aquatic life teeming just a few feet below us. We saw brightly colored fish, gently swaying plants, and, of course, the coral reef itself—alive with activity. It was truly a wow experience.

At some point, I decided to lift my head out of the water and look around. I gasped. Caught in a riptide, we had drifted more than a mile out to sea. The shoreline looked impossibly far away. Our hotel—all the hotels—looked like toys in the distance.

I immediately shouted to Gail who, fortunately, was still just a few feet from me. She looked up, saw our predicament, and then looked at me in near panic. "Oh my gosh. What are we going to do?"

Fortunately, we had a boogie board with us, on which we had planned to place shells and other items we hoped to find on the ocean floor. We both grabbed on to it and started paddling for our lives—literally.

We swam for more than an hour. Eventually, as we neared the shore, we stood up in the shallow water. We trudged up to the beach and collapsed in the sand. We were utterly exhausted. We realized just how close we had come to disaster. This was not the outcome we had intended when we innocently slipped into the water that morning.

So much of life is similar to this experience. You start out with one thing in mind and then, without consciously intending to do so, end up in an entirely different location. It is the power of *the drift*.

Now think of drift in the context of creating a product, service, or cause.

If you've worked in the corporate world, you've attended that first Big Vision Meeting. Someone has a dream for an exciting and compelling product. This is how many wow products are born. People are energized. The creative spigot is turned on. The ideas flow. The room is alive with possibility.

But then we come to the second meeting. A few people report on the assignments they were given. Maybe they share a sketch, a proposal, or a demo. It's not bad; in fact, it's pretty good. But it just doesn't quite match up with our expectations. Something is missing.

Everyone is polite. A few even make suggestions. But somewhere deep inside you realize that the dream has taken a hit. It hasn't died, of course. But it has been dialed back—calibrated to the reality of deadlines, budgets, and limited resources.

A similar process can happen for individuals who set out to create something, whether a book, a record album, or even a comedy routine. It's easy to "settle."

At this very moment, you face a decision. Will you take a stand for the original vision or will you—and everyone else in the room—be swept out to sea, drifting along with the current, oblivious to what is happening?

Here are six ways to find the courage you need to make "wow" happen.

1. **Take a stand for greatness**. Like many important things in life, creating a wow experience begins with making a commitment. You must resolve in your own heart that you will not sell out or settle. This isn't necessary for every project, of course. But when you decide that the dream warrants it, you have to take a stand and play full-out.

2. **Connect with the original vision.** King Solomon once said, "Where there is no vision, the people perish."[1] This is also true for wow. Before it exists, it is only an idea. The only place it exists is inside your head. Sometimes you just have to close your eyes and once again become present to what it is you are trying to create.
3. **Remind yourself what is at stake.** I have found that the best way to do this is to ask, "Why is this so important?" When I was writing my first book, I had a list of seven reasons why I needed to write the book. I reviewed it every morning before I began writing. It gave the project an almost epic significance, but it kept me going when I wanted to quit.
4. **Listen to your heart.** Most of us have spent a lifetime ignoring—or even suppressing—our intuition. I don't know if this is a product of modern rationalism or American pragmatism. Regardless, I believe intuition is the map to buried treasure. It is not infallible, but neither is our reason. And it can point us in the right direction. We need to pay attention to this inner voice.
5. **Speak up.** This is the crucial step. You must give voice to your heart and go on the record to defend your wow ideas. If you don't, who will? You may be the original dream's last best chance of staying alive. This is why you can't afford to remain silent.
6. **Be stubborn.** This is perhaps the toughest part of all. We all want to be liked. We don't want to be "high maintenance" or unreasonable. But think back on your own history. Aren't the people you respect the most also the ones who demanded the most from you? You may not have fully appreciated it at the time but, looking back, their stubborn refusal to settle is what made the difference.

The truth is, mediocrity is natural. You don't have to do anything to drift there. It just happens. But if you want to create truly wow experiences—and if you want to build your platform—then it is going to require courage. Are you willing to be brave?

SIX

Give Your Product a Memorable Name

Sooner or later, you will have to give your wow product or service a name that will help it connect with the potential prospect. This is the case for your naming your blog as well. Your pet name for your product must be ruthlessly eliminated. Because what you call it is more than just a title: it's your number one marketing tool.

Igor, a naming and branding company, has titled everything from TruTV to the Nokia Evolve phone. They know the secret to successfully connecting to customers. In a commentary about the Yahoo! Personals tagline,[1] "Believe," the folks at Igor said:

> "Believe" is a masterful example of how to achieve the brass ring of branding: Engagement. A less savvy tagline might have been "Find that special someone you have always dreamed about," but that approach would be far less effective because it:
>
> - is exactly what people would expect to hear and would pass through them like white noise.
> - narrowly defines the Yahoo! Personals as merely a service offering.
> - tells the audience how to think about it, with no room left for mystery.
>
> "Believe" is a home run for their tagline because it:

- causes people to pause and ask themselves "Believe in what?" and to actively fill in the blanks and personalize the connection, which is the most effective form of engagement.

- elevates the Yahoo! Personals brand above the goods and services they offer and taps into a positive aspirational philosophy.[2]

Igor says this strategy is also demonstrated by these taglines: Nike's "Just Do It," Apple's "Think Different," Fannie Mae's "We're in the American Dream Business," or Guidant's "It's a Great Time to Be Alive."[3]

Coming up with compelling names for products, services, blogs, and blog headlines is arduous, time-consuming work. Yet nothing in the marketing mix is more important than a strong title. It is like a newspaper headline: If prospective readers are intrigued, they keep reading. If they don't, they move on to the next thing that catches their attention.

Based on the research we did while I was at Thomas Nelson Publishers, I know that what you name your product (in our case, books) is one of the most important things you do. Consumers first look at the book's title, then the front and back covers and the flaps. Rounding out the list are the table of contents, the first few paragraphs of the book, and the price.

The most important component for anything you offer is the title.

So what does it take to create titles that make your product a best seller, generate page views for a blog post, or generate interest in your service?

Great titles are PINC (pronounced "pink"). They do at least one of the following: make a *promise*, create *intrigue*, identify a *need*, or simply state the *content*. Let me provide a few examples.

P: Titles that make a promise. For example:

- *The 4-Hour Body: An Uncommon Guide to Rapid Fat-Loss, Incredible Sex, and Becoming Superhuman* (book)
- *POWER 90: Tony Horton's Total Body Transformation 90 Day Boot Camp Workout* (DVDs)

- Omega Paw Self-Cleaning Litter Box (for cats)

I: Titles that create intrigue. For example:

- *Steve Jobs: One Last Thing* (movie)
- *Heaven Is for Real: A Little Boy's Astounding Story of His Trip to Heaven and Back* (book)
- Euphoria, by Calvin Klein, eau de parfum spray (perfumes)

N: Titles that identify a need. For example:

- Mommy I'm Here Child Locator (wireless GPS bracelet for kids)
- True Calm Amino Relaxer by New Foods (supplement)
- *Fearless: Imagine Your Life Without Fear* (book)

C: Titles that simply state the content. For example:

- College Hunks Hauling Junk (service)
- *Autobiography of Mark Twain, Vol. 1* (book)
- Joe's Plumbing, Heating, and Air Conditioning, LLC (repair service)

Some of these titles employ more than one strategy. For example, *The 4-Hour Body* makes a promise, but it also creates intrigue—how could you re-create your body in four hours?[4]

And I have to admit that many books and other products break these rules completely and succeed. I remember trying to come up with a title for *Blue Like Jazz* by Donald Miller. Our committee was convinced that the author's title would never work. We believed that no one would have a clue what it meant.

But Don was stubborn and wouldn't budge. We finally acquiesced. And all it did was work! The book has sold more than 1.3 million copies at this writing and still continues to sell tens of thousands of copies each year.

By the way, one of the best books bloggers could ever read is David Garfinkel's *Advertising Headlines That Make You Rich*.[5] It is basically a catalog of headline templates that have proven effective in selling all kinds of products.

The bottom line is the right title for your product, service, website, or blog can make you or break you. It is worth spending the necessary time to get it right.

SEVEN

Wrap the Wow in Style

While people shouldn't judge a book or any other product by its cover, they do. This is why it is so critical that you spend the time and money to get the packaging on your product right. It doesn't matter if it's a dog toy, a clothing line, a book, or a record album. People will never get to experience your brilliance unless the packaging gets them to pick it up and explore it.

This is especially important in today's world. As we've discussed, you have never had more competition. The market is increasingly crowded—and noisy. You need every advantage you can muster. Packaging is a key component in the selling process. This is often where the war for the consumer's mind is won or lost.

I am not a designer but have worked with hundreds of them over the span of my career. I have been responsible for hiring them, evaluating their work, and picking the designs that I thought would work. Along with some tremendous successes have come a few abysmal failures. I've learned from both.

With this perspective, here are ten tips for developing eye-popping packaging and thus increasing your chances of sales success:

1. **Know your audience.** A while ago, I had to speak to a group of college students. I hired a design firm to prepare my slides. When I got them back, I didn't care for the design. Then I showed them to my two college-age daughters. They loved them, and the slides were a big hit

with my audience. The point is that it's not about you. It's about your audience. What would *they* find compelling?

2. **Consider your brand.** While the audience is important, so is your brand. You have to strike a balance between reaching your audience and representing who you are—or want to become. This means paying close attention to fonts, colors, and even textures and materials. All of them communicate subtle messages about your brand.

3. **Review the best-seller lists.** It is worth taking a look at the best sellers in your product category. What current design trends do you see? What seems to be working? Review the top one hundred products and take notes. For example, as I wrote this book, I reviewed the top business books and took copious notes. This has expanded my design horizons and stimulated my thinking.

4. **Make the investment necessary.** You won't get a second chance to make a first impression. If your packaging looks cheap, dated, or confusing, your prospective customers will assume that your actual product is (surprise!) cheap, dated, or confusing. Therefore, you need to invest in the best designer you can afford. Don't try to do it yourself to save money (unless you are actually a designer). Remember, there is nothing more expensive than a cheap design that doesn't work.

5. **Don't provide too much direction—at least initially.** Don't limit the imagination of your designers. If you do, you won't get their best work. Instead, describe your product and the audience. Then get out of the way and see what they come up with.

6. **Insist on several comps.** Tell designers up front that you will want to see several comps (short for "comprehensive layouts"). You want to be able to pick and choose from various alternatives. I often find that I like the type on one version, the illustration on another, and the color selection on yet another. If you and the designer limit yourself to one option, you will find that you often get stuck and have a tough time moving forward without friction.

7. **Be careful with design metaphors.** By this I mean the illustration or photo you use to represent your message or story. For example, sitting on my desk right now are books with cover illustrations of a chair, a chess game, a light bulb, a sunset, and an elephant trunk. Some of these are perfect. Others leave me scratching my head. If you use a design metaphor, make sure the connection to the product is obvious. Think about all the messages it communicates.
8. **Don't let the design get in the way.** My favorite designs are those that are simple and elegant. They are kind of like the drum track on a great song. You'd miss it if it wasn't there, but you barely notice it when it is. Or to say it another way, the design doesn't compete with the message for attention; instead, it facilitates it. Be especially wary of designs that require an explanation for you to "get it." Your prospective customers won't have the benefit of someone standing next to them in the store or online explaining what it means.
9. **Evaluate the packaging in context.** Once you are close to a final design, you need to evaluate it in the various merchandising environments in which your product will appear. For example, will the packaging "pop" on a shelf with similar items? Is the type readable from five feet away? What about ten? What about the online context? How will it look when it is reduced to 260 pixels high on an online retailer site? Don't get married to a design until you have seen the product in the appropriate environments.
10. **Ask your fans.** If you already have a blog, Twitter, or Facebook following, you can test various design options with your best prospects—the people who already want to hear what you have to say. You can use a service like SurveyMonkey[1] to display cover options and then let your fans vote. That's exactly how this book ended up with the cover design it has. I placed this cover, plus several other strong options, on SurveyMonkey and created a blog posting to allow people to vote directly from my blog. Who better to ask than people who are already engaged with your message? It's also helpful if they can comment, because they will offer other options or see things you may have missed. This is crowdsourcing at its best!

Don't underestimate the importance of great design. When it comes to selling your product, it can make you or break you.

═══

You're about to graduate from this short course on creating, naming, and packaging a wow product. I sincerely hope I've convinced you that this first element in the success formula is an absolute must. A compelling product *plus* a significant platform *equals* a big win for you.

PART TWO

PREPARE TO LAUNCH

EIGHT

Accept Personal Responsibility

Marketing entrepreneur Yolanda Allen tells an amusing story in an article on BetterNetworker.com. It seems her daughter, Makaila, decided to make herself some french fries for dinner one night. "She doesn't like anyone eating her food," wrote Yolanda, "especially if she's cooking it for herself." The story continues:

> So she asked me to let her know if anyone started to eat her fries, which were cooking, because she had to go do something. I was in the middle of listening to a webinar and taking notes.
>
> Now I must tell you that one of the reasons I retired from the Air Force is that I wanted to be available for my children. But my daughter thinks that I'm at her beck and call ALL THE TIME.
>
> I had had a very busy day which was full of interruptions already, so I was a "little bit" annoyed when she asked me to watch her fries. I replied, probably with a look of disgust, with "Makaila, I'm NOT babysitting your french fries." You should have seen the look on her face. She was speechless, and Makaila loves to talk . . . too much.[1]

Yolanda followed this up with a question to her readers: are you taking responsibility for running your business . . . or are you asking someone to babysit your business?

Makaila is a little like many of us. We have the wow product—the fries—but we don't want the full responsibility that entails. Let me ask you a question: are you prepared to take full personal responsibility for building your own platform, or are you thinking of hiring a babysitter? If the answer is a wobbly "I guess I'll do it," then ask yourself why.

Are you afraid because you don't know what you're doing? Let me assure you you're not alone. It can seem a daunting and complex task. This section will give you the hammer and nails you'll need to have on hand before you begin constructing your platform.

I've spoken to many people just starting out who think they can hire out the responsibility to someone who knows more about marketing than they do. *Someone with experience*, they think. *Yeah*, that's *what I need!*

But I can assure you this is not something you can afford to leave to others. You must take responsibility for it yourself. There are four primary reasons why this is necessary:

1. **No one knows your product better than you do.** Even if you are fortunate enough to have a company that markets your products, or you can afford to hire a marketing firm, they will never have the nuts-and-bolts knowledge of your product or service that you do.
2. **No one is more passionate about your product than you are.** Do you really think anyone could care about your offering more than you? I doubt it. You took months—perhaps years—to develop it. You kept going when that little voice in your head told you that you were crazy. You endured a string of rejections. But you kept going. Why? *Love.* You were passionate about your product or service or message. You just had to share it with the world.
3. **No one has more skin in the game than you do.** If your offering fails, the marketing firm employee handling your account will go on to the next project. The company distributing your product will fill that product slot with something else. The speaker's bureau will find another person to talk on the same topic you did. It is not that they don't care; it's just that their bets are spread across a portfolio of projects. Not so with you. Your fortunes rise or fall on the success of your current project. If it succeeds, you reap the lion's share of the rewards. If it fails, you suffer the consequences. Your career is on the line.

4. **No one is likely to do it if you don't.** I wish this weren't the case, but for 95 percent of us it is.

This is why you must take matters into your own hands. Don't let someone else babysit your french fries. Let me suggest that you take a long look in the mirror. The person you are looking at is your new chief marketing officer. Take responsibility for your own success and invite others to join you in the endeavor.

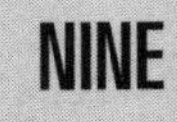

Think Bigger . . . No, *Bigger*!

While you are preparing to launch, consider your mental attitude. If you're going to be the chief marketing officer for your wow product, you must think bigger than you ever have before. On my blog I wrote once about how the mind-set of successful creatives—authors, speakers, musicians, and so on—differ from less successful ones. I listed *thinking big* as the number one characteristic. Several of my readers commented that they struggled with this.

I certainly understand why. When we are young, parents and teachers tell us we can do anything and become whatever we want. But as we grow older, these same people tell us we must be more realistic.

Pretty soon, their collective voices become our internal naysayer. As soon as we have a big thought, we check ourselves: *C'mon. Get real. That will never happen. You have to be more realistic*. And so it goes. We mistake this for wisdom.

That was the mind-set I had until I picked up *The Magic of Thinking Big* by David Schwartz.[1] This book was originally published in 1959. I read it for the first time in the late '80s. It forever changed my approach to life and work.

Since that time, I have become convinced that thinking big is not a gift but a skill—one that anyone can develop. It starts by understanding the process and then consistently practicing it. If you are going to build a successful platform, you need this skill too.

Here are seven steps to thinking big:

1. **Imagine the possibilities.** Give yourself permission to dream. I remember doing this when I was writing my first book. I imagined what it would be like to be a best-selling author. I thought about what it would be like to see my book on the *New York Times* bestsellers list.

2. **Write down your dream.** This is the act that transforms a dream into a goal. Wonderful things happen when you commit something to writing. I don't fully understand how it works, but I have experienced it firsthand again and again. The phenomenon is explained in a very compelling book by Henriette Anne Klauser called *Write It Down, Make It Happen.*[2] She used the example of Lou Holtz.

   As a young man in 1966, Holtz wrote down his personal and professional goals one evening. They seemed impossible. He was broke and unemployed, and his wife was about to have their third child. Klauser said:

   > His list included having dinner at the White House, appearing on *The Tonight Show*, meeting the pope, becoming head coach at Notre Dame, winning a national championship, being coach of the year, landing on an aircraft carrier, making a hole in one, and jumping out of an airplane. . . .
   >
   > If you check Coach Lou Holtz's website, along with the list you will get pictures—pictures of Holtz with the pope, with President Reagan at the White House, yukking it up with Johnny Carson. In addition, a description of what it was like to jump out of an airplane and get not one but two holes in one.[3]

   To date he has achieved 102 of his original 107 goals.

3. **Connect with what is at stake.** This is your rationale. Unfortunately, it is a crucial step that people often omit. Before you can find your way, you must discover your *why*. Why is this goal important to you? What will achieving it make possible? What is at stake if you don't? What will you have to give up in order to achieve it? Your rationale

provides the intellectual and emotional power to keep going when the path becomes difficult. (And it will.)

4. **Outline what would have to be true.** Rather than merely asking how to get from where you are to where you want to go (strategy), I like asking what would have to be true for my dream to become a reality. For example, when I set a goal of hitting the best-sellers list, I realized I would have to write a compelling book, become its chief spokesperson, get major media exposure, and so forth. I started with the dream and worked backward.
5. **Decide what you can do to affect the outcome.** This is where you transition from the big picture to daily actions. This is where people often get derailed. They can't see all the steps that will take them to their goal. So rather than doing something, they do nothing. *You will never see the full path.* The important thing is to do the next right thing. What can you do today to move you toward your dream?
6. **Determine when this will happen.** Someone once said a goal is simply a dream with a deadline. A deadline is one way to make the dream more concrete—which is exactly what thinking big is about. A deadline also creates a sense of urgency that will motivate you to take action. Force yourself to assign a "by when" date to every goal. (If you get stuck, ask yourself, *What's the worst that can happen if I don't hit this?*)
7. **Review your goals daily.** When I was writing my first book, I reviewed my goals daily. I prayed over them. I determined what I needed to do today to make them a reality. It gave me a laser focus, especially when the dream looked impossible—when the publisher called to cancel the contract, when my publicist told me no one was interested in the book, when the publisher ran out of inventory right after the book hit the best-sellers list. (This all happened, by the way.)

Don't listen to that mocking little voice that tells you to be more realistic. Ignore it. You can either accept reality as it is or create it as you wish it to be. This is the essence of dreaming—and thinking big.

TEN

Define Your Platform Goals

When you think about building a powerful platform, what does it look like? Can you describe it in detail? One of the most important things you can do to ensure you launch well is to get your plans out of your head and down on paper.

For years I have written my goals on yellow legal pads, on black notebooks, in special goal-setting software, and now in the digital application called Evernote. Here are just a few goals I have written down over the last four decades:

- Marry a strong, loving woman who is passionate about hospitality.
- Make one hundred thousand dollars a year doing what I love.
- Lose twenty-five pounds and complete a half marathon.
- Write a *New York Times* best-selling book.
- Become the CEO of Thomas Nelson Publishers.

Of course, most people don't bother to write down their goals. Instead, they drift through life aimlessly, wondering why their life lacks purpose and significance. I am not saying that committing your goals to writing is the endgame. It's not. But it is the beginning.

Here are five reasons you should commit your platform goals to writing:

1. **Because it will force you to clarify what you want.** Dave Ramsey, author of *The Total Money Makeover*, helps people who want to become

debt-free to be crystal clear on their goals. Every credit card balance, each car loan, every dollar they spend—everything—must be written down and tracked constantly. Why? It forces them to be certain about their goals. Ramsey calls it "gazelle intensity."

He got the term from watching a program about how cheetahs stalk gazelles. While the cheetah is the fastest animal on land, it only catches a gazelle about one in nineteen times. "Around our office," he says, "the counselors can predict who will make it out of debt based on how 'gazelle-intense' they are."[1] Writing down your platform goals can help you clarify what they are so you can become "gazelle intense" about achieving them.

2. **Because it will motivate you to take action.** Writing your platform goals down is only the beginning. You must execute on your goals. You have to take action. I have found that writing down my goals and reviewing them regularly provokes me to take the next most important action.
3. **Because it will provide a filter for other opportunities.** The more successful you become, the more you will be deluged with opportunities. In fact, these new opportunities can quickly become distractions that pull you off course. The only antidote I know of is to maintain a list of written goals by which to evaluate these new opportunities.
4. **Because it will help you overcome resistance.** Every meaningful intention encounters resistance. From the moment you set a goal, you will begin to feel it. But if you focus on the resistance, it will only get stronger. The only way I have found for overcoming this is to focus on the goal. Steven Pressfield's book *Do the Work* is must reading on this topic.[2]
5. **Because it will enable you to see—and celebrate—your progress.** Life is hard when you aren't seeing progress. You feel like you are going nowhere. But written goals are like mile markers on a highway. They enable you to see how far you have come and how far you need to go. They also provide an opportunity for celebration when you attain them.

Writing your platform goals down doesn't take that long. Don't overthink the process. Just get something on paper and refine it as you go. I think you will find that the benefits are well worth the effort.

ELEVEN

Create an Elevator Pitch

Part of launching successfully is being prepared to present your idea—your product, your service, or your cause—succinctly. To do that, you need to create an "elevator pitch." This is a short summary of your product offering, including your target market (the people most likely to become your customers) and your value proposition (what you have to offer those customers).

The name comes from the idea that you should be able to deliver a short, compelling description of what you offer in the time it takes to ride an elevator up a few floors—approximately thirty seconds to two minutes.

As important as the elevator speech was in past years, it's become more crucial to get it right online, where you have even less time to grab the attention of a potential customer than you would have in an actual elevator. Most people's focused attention span—the kind that is a short-term response to stimulus—is very brief, with a maximum span, without any lapse at all, as short as eight seconds.[1]

When you don't have an exciting and concise elevator speech, you will fail to connect with your potential customers and you will lose business. Why handicap your platform-building goals before you even get started?

Aileen Pincus, president of the Pincus Group, an executive coaching firm, hears a lot of elevator pitches. At a conference years ago, a young businesswoman approached Pincus to introduce herself and her Web-building services. "She was eager and confident," says Pincus, "but after a few minutes of hearing about her competitive pricing, her creativity, and a few of her clients, I said: 'Well I hear from a lot of design services, and it's hard to tell the real differences between you. What do you think really sets your work apart for someone like me in a services industry?'"

The question caught the young woman off guard. "She admitted she didn't have an answer. An honest answer, but not a first impression that achieved her goal of getting a second meeting."[2]

People with successful platforms have often spent hours honing and practicing their elevator pitches. The stakes are huge. If they are successful and connect with a potential customer, they win the opportunity to take the next step, whether that is a potential product sale, a booking for their seminar, or time to present their message. If they don't, they are sent packing like the young woman Aileen Pincus met.

Why do you need an elevator pitch? Here are my three top reasons:

1. **It forces you to achieve clarity yourself.** As a former book publisher, I can't tell you how many authors I have spoken with over the years who could not summarize what their book was about. They should have achieved clarity on this before they began writing. You simply must be able to succinctly state what your product does, what your service provides, or what your seminar teaches. If not, you'll be hearing a lot of nos. It is also why you should strive for a clear elevator pitch before you do anything else.
2. **It helps you understand your customers' perspective.** If you are going to connect with your potential customers, you must see your offering from their perspective. Moreover, you must understand their problems, their concerns, their hopes, and their dreams. Only then can you put together an offering they will find compelling.
3. **It provides a tool for enrolling strategic partners.** In order to be successful in launching anything significant, you need help. You can't do it all yourself. Whether you are talking to a publisher, a record company, a booking agent, a publicist, a retailer, or a corporate sponsor, you need to be able to explain quickly what you are about. Only then can your potential partner decide whether or not he or she can help you.

Okay, so you're convinced. But how do you craft a good elevator pitch?

First, understand the pitch will be different depending on whether you are offering an *information* product (e.g., nonfiction book, speech, consulting service, and so on) or an *entertainment* product (e.g., novel, screenplay, comedy act, or other diversions). Note that when I use the term *product*, I am referring to your creative output regardless of the form. It could be an actual product, a service, or even a cause.

An elevator pitch for an information product should consist of four components:

1. Your product name and category
2. The problem you are attempting to solve
3. Your proposed solution
4. The key benefit of your solution

Here's an example of how I pitched this book:

> I am writing a new [Component 1] business book called *Platform*. [Component 2] It is designed for anyone who is trying to get attention for his or her product, service, or cause. [Component 3] I teach my readers how to build a tribe of loyal followers, using social media and other new technologies. [Component 4] I explain that it has never been easier, less expensive, or more possible than right now.

An elevator pitch for an entertainment product should also consist of four components:

1. Your product name and category
2. The main character's ambition
3. The conflict he or she encounters
4. The real significance of the story

Here's an example from a mythical project about the modern composer, Eric Whitacre:

> I am shooting an [Component 1] inspirational documentary called *Cloudburst.* [Component 2] It is about a young, extremely gifted musician who dreams of becoming a symphony conductor. [Component 3] The only problem is he can't read music. As a result, no one in the music business will give him a chance. [Component 4] Yet he ultimately succeeds because of his honesty, optimism, and hard work.

Obviously, pitches can vary widely, depending on your offering. Regardless, you want to create an elevator pitch that is clear and compelling. This is a prerequisite to attracting the partners and prospects you need to succeed.

By the way, once you get your elevator pitch fine-tuned, don't deliver it like a mechanical parrot. Instead, do what Michael Port suggests in chapter 4 of his excellent book *Book Yourself Solid*: use it as the foundation of a meaningful conversation.[3]

TWELVE

Set Up Your Branding Tools

If there's a handyman in your life, he or she may already have one of the popular Leatherman multi-tools. But if you want to give him a special gift, you need look no further than the limited-edition 18-karat gold Del Ray Leatherman tool created by artist Adrian Pallarols.[1] It's only a cool forty thousand dollars! If, like me, you missed out on buying one of the twenty-five created, relax. You're preparing to launch your platform and build your brand, so your multi-tool will look a little different.

You may be overlooking some of the simple tools already at your disposal. Literally, every point of contact is an opportunity to create a positive brand impression—if you are intentional.

Here are five basic personal branding tools you should take advantage of before you move on to more complex ones.

1. **E-mail Address**. The other day I received an e-mail message from someone who claimed to be a social media expert, specializing in personal branding. Only problem was that his e-mail address was something like rooster763@aol.com. That instantly killed his credibility with me.

   If you are using an AOL e-mail address, stop. Nothing screams "I am stuck in the '90s!" like AOL. The same is true for yahoo.com and hotmail.com. The only exception is Gmail. Use this format: firstname.lastname@gmail.com. This looks way more professional than lovecat23@gmail.com.

   Better yet, buy your own domain name for ten to twenty dollars per year. You will have an e-mail address that looks like this:

yourname@yourdomain.com. This makes a positive, powerful brand impression.

2. **E-mail Signature**. Your e-mail signature is an opportunity to create another branding impression. But be careful. If you include too much information, it just becomes a big, gnarly ad. If you include too little, you miss a great opportunity.

Ask yourself what information people really need about you. Maybe they need your phone number. Or maybe they don't. (I don't provide mine, because I don't want anyone calling me who doesn't already have my number.)

It's a good idea to include links to your blog or website, links to your social media profiles, and perhaps a mention of your newest project. (Don't overdo it.) I also include a disclaimer at the bottom.

Here's my current signature:

Michael Hyatt

MY BLOG http://michaelhyatt.com
SPEAKING http://michaelhyatt.com/speaking
TWITTER http://twitter.com/michaelhyatt
FACEBOOK http://www.facebook.com/michaelhyatt
GOOGLE+ http://gplus.to/michaelhyatt

:: This email is off the record (blogs and tweets too) unless we agree otherwise. ::

(Thanks to Seth Godin for the disclaimer at the end of the signature.)

3. **Business Cards**. This is another way to create a powerful branding impression and also pass along important information. It is astonishing how creative people are with this. But don't go overboard.

Communicate the basics: your logo, your name, contact information, and perhaps a tagline. Make sure to include your social media contact information. I have seen some cards with just a Twitter username or a website address. That can be effective too, depending on your purpose.

You can do this yourself with software like Photoshop or (my favorite) Acorn.[2] (If you want a dedicated software program, try Business

Card Composer.[3]) If you want to kick-start your creativity, here are hundreds of creative examples from a website called CardFaves.[4]

4. **Website.** This is undoubtedly the single most important branding tool you can have. It is the first way in which most people will encounter you. It will shape their opinion of you. That's why you must get it right. I will spend several chapters talking about it in the next section.

   Hire a web designer if you can afford one. Talk to him or her about what you want to communicate. Write down a few words you hope visitors will use to describe you. Pay attention to colors and fonts. These all communicate in subtle ways.

   If you can't afford a web designer yet, at least start with a professionally created "theme," or look. When I moved to WordPress, I started with WooThemes.[5] I have family members and friends who use ElegantThemes.[6] I am currently using a customized version of Standard Theme,[7] which I love. You can purchase a great theme for fifty to one hundred dollars.

5. **Social Media Profiles.** Once you have a look for your blog or web page, incorporate as many elements of the theme as you can into your social media profiles. Twitter, Facebook, YouTube, and others allow you to customize the background graphics and other elements.

   The goal is for your fans and followers to have a consistent brand experience. Use the same logo, color palette, and fonts on every platform. You want them to land on one of your social media profiles and know instantly that it is your profile.

   I hired TweetPages[8] to design mine. It was a couple hundred dollars to have them design a custom background for my Twitter, Facebook, and YouTube pages. For a high-quality graphic artist, this was a bargain. As a bonus, it was one of the best customer service experiences I've ever had.

These five tools can go a long way toward creating a positive first or second impression. Don't think of them in isolation, but rather as part of your overall brand-management and platform-building program. And the good news is that while you won't own a limited-edition gold Leatherman tool, they won't run you forty thousand bucks.

THIRTEEN

Assemble Your Pit Crew

Although you are the one who must be responsible for building your platform, you still need a team. You can't go it alone. The job is just too big. You may have to start small, but you have to enroll others to help you get to your destination. Plan this before you launch and have your team as complete as possible.

In his book *Get Off Your "But,"* author Sean Stephenson shares the concept of assembling a pit crew, as is done in auto racing.[1] This is a helpful metaphor for thinking about your professional career. In essence, you are the race car driver. Your message or product is the car. You must take personal responsibility for the outcome. But you won't get far without a pit crew.

In a car race, the pit crew is responsible for optimizing the vehicle and keeping everything running smoothly; each person has a narrowly defined role. This frees the driver to do the job that only he or she can do. The pit crew keeps the car on the track and in the race.

In building a platform, the same thing is true. You need a team of folks whose specialized roles allow you to do what you do best. Here are some of the teammates you may need to recruit as you build your platform.

ADMINISTRATION

Administrative help frees you to focus on what you do best: create. At some point, you may need to hire one or more of the following:

- **Assistant.** Is it really a good use of your time to process e-mail, make travel arrangements, and respond to meeting requests? This doesn't have to be a full-time position. I hired a virtual assistant through EAHelp.com for fifteen hours per week.[2] I couldn't be happier with my decision.
- **Bookkeeper.** Just because you can keep your own books doesn't mean you should. Again, this is time away from creating. Also, like a virtual assistant, you can hire someone part-time. I have someone who does this a few hours a month. Like an assistant, it frees me up to do what only I can do.
- **Attorney.** The more successful you become, the more you will need a good, reliable attorney. Not all attorneys are created equal, however. You need one that specializes in intellectual property.

MANAGEMENT

Management is the term used to refer to the person or company who manages your overall career and helps develop your platform. There are basically two options:

- **Self-Management.** This is what almost all creatives do. You are, in essence, your own "general contractor." You hire the subs and manage them. At some point, this starts diffusing your focus and eating into your creative time. But in the meantime, you must take responsibility for this. It is not the role of your literary agent, booking agent, or some other professional.
- **Personal Management.** The most successful creatives hire a personal manager to oversee their career. The good news is you typically pay a percentage of your income (or, better for you, gross profit), so the manager only makes more money if you make more money. The bad news is it is difficult to find someone who has the necessary experience and is also competent and trustworthy.

REPRESENTATION

Agents represent you to potential customers for your work. They are different than managers. Think of them as salespeople. Generally, they report to managers. They are the linkage connecting you to the people you need to get the word out. In hiring an agent you need someone who will represent you well, since others will form their opinion of you based on their interactions with your agent(s).

- **Literary Agent.** This is a must-have for authors. You generally can't get in the publishing door without one. Why? Because traditional publishers use agents as filters to separate the wheat from the chaff. It also provides the clout you need in the contract negotiation process. Publishers aren't out to take advantage of you, but they are naturally focused on their own interests.
- **Booking Agent.** This is a must-have for speakers or other entertainers. A good booking agent can give you access to event planners you wouldn't have otherwise. He can generally get you a higher fee than you would on your own. (Most people aren't good at negotiating for themselves.) He or she can also make sure your intellectual property rights are protected and that you have the production quality you need (e.g., sound, lights, and so on) to do your best.
- **Publicity Agent.** Regardless of whether you are an author, comedian, speaker, or some other kind of creative, you will likely need a publicist at some point. This is especially true when you are launching a new product. Unlike literary agents and booking agents, most publicists work on a fee basis rather than on a commission. However, you can usually hire them on a per-project basis.

CONTENT CREATION

These are the people who help you create your content. I don't recommend having them create it for you, but they can definitely assist:

- **Coaches**. Wherever it is you want to go, someone has likely been there before. Some of these people have become skilled coaches as well. I have used them to help me get better in specific areas. For example, you might consider hiring a writing coach, speech coach, or a voice coach. It doesn't have to be expensive, and it can be temporary. You might just need someone to get you to the next level.
- **Collaborators**. These are people who help you get your content into marketable shape. This could be as simple as an editor but might include a ghostwriter—or something in between. If you are producing audio or video, it might be a producer or video editor. The options are limitless. The point is you don't have to do it all yourself. It's always a smart idea to have a professional—producer, editor, copywriter, or other industry professional—look over your work to be sure it's up to snuff.

PUBLISHERS

These are the individuals or companies that help you get your product to market. The word *publish* means "to make known." It might be a book publisher, a video distributor, or an online retailer. You might even do it yourself (e.g., self-publishing). Regardless, you have to consider publishers as part of your team.

To summarize, if you are serious about getting your work out, you need to begin building a pit crew. Why? Because it provides three benefits:

1. Access to contacts you don't have.
2. Leverage that maximizes your impact.
3. Freedom to focus on what you do best.

You may have to start small (everyone does), but this overview will help you prioritize so you can build the team you need to accomplish the results you want.

FOURTEEN

Secure Raving Endorsements

A selection of endorsements of you and/or your product or service is absolutely essential for a strong platform. Endorsements are used extensively in all forms of marketing—and for good reason. They provide third-party validation and social authority. They make it easier for potential gatekeepers and customers to say yes.

Easy access to social media, review sites, and product comments means we depend more and more on what other people say about a product or service before we make a purchase. If several people you respect recommend a product, you may make your purchasing decision on that alone.

In fact, you have probably endorsed something recently yourself. If you've "liked" something on Facebook, you have effectively endorsed it.

The power of this simple click is evident in a December 2011 joint survey conducted by ReverbNation and Digital Music News. They found that musicians now regard Facebook likes (48.13 percent) as being three times as valuable as e-mail sign-ups (14.03 percent). And they made similar comparisons to YouTube channel (15.90 percent) subscribers and Twitter followers (14.45 percent).[1]

Relying on endorsements has become commonplace in almost every area of life. Why? Because with so many options, few of us have time to do the evaluation ourselves. Instead, we rely on the opinions of people we trust. This reduces the risk and helps us make a decision more quickly.

This is why—if you are going to build a successful platform—you can't afford to ignore endorsements. You must try to get them for every product or service you create. While the process is sometimes difficult and time-consuming, it is absolutely crucial to getting the visibility and credibility you need.

Endorsements fall into one of two types:

1. **Celebrity Endorsements.** These don't have to be movie or television personalities. They may simply be the well-known experts in a narrow field. For example, if I wanted to buy a new pair of running shoes and saw an endorsement from Christopher McDougall, that would mean something to me, because he is a leading authority on barefoot running.[2]
2. **User Reviews.** These are important too. I want to know what kind of experience mere mortals have had with the product or service. The celebrity endorser may have all kinds of motives for endorsing a product or service, but individuals are more likely to be candid.

By the way, some negative reviews from ordinary users can be helpful. If all user reviews are positive, I get suspicious. When a few are negative, I assume they are all honest and put greater stock in the positive ones.

So how do you get endorsements? Here are the five steps I recommend:

1. **Create a great product.** I spent the entire last section of the book on this, but it is worth repeating. People who matter are not going to endorse a mediocre product. They can't afford to. Why? Because their brand will be hurt by the negative association. So you must be committed to excellence. (Note: I did not say *perfection*. You do the best you can, then launch.)
2. **Make a prospect list.** In an ideal world, whom would you like as endorsers? Think big. (When I wrote my e-book *Creating Your Personal Life Plan*,[3] I started with a list of forty people. I ended up getting endorsements from twenty-five of them.) Ask yourself, *Who are the recognized authorities in my field?* Don't be too quick to rule out someone because you don't think you have access. You may not know the prospective endorser, but you may know someone who does.

3. **Leverage one endorsement for more.** It's always difficult to go first. Sometimes prospective endorsers need an endorsement themselves in order to get comfortable with your product.

   With my e-book, I looked over the list and said, "Who is the most likely to say yes because of my relationship with him or her?" I then asked this person for an endorsement. Sure enough, I got it. I included that endorsement in all my other requests. (It also gave me the courage to ask the others.) This made it easier for everyone, because someone else had already gone first.

4. **Ask for the endorsement.** Don't beat around the bush. Busy people—like the ones you want endorsements from—don't have time to read long e-mails. Get to the point. Also, try to ask them when they would be the most receptive. For example, I always ask for speaking endorsements (and I always ask for them) right after the engagement, while it is fresh on their minds and before they get too distracted with everything else.

5. **Provide guidance, samples, and a deadline.** Include a brief description of your product and perhaps a sample. Then offer to send them the entire product. Tell them the kind of endorsement you are looking for. The more specific, the better.

   I always tell them I am just looking for two to three sentences. They might write more, but this sounds doable. I then provide a real endorsement or two and a deadline. I ask for it within a week. In my experience you are more likely to get an endorsement with a short deadline rather than a longer one.

When you get the endorsement, thank the endorser and then display the endorsements prominently on your product and in your marketing. I have also started distilling the endorsements into sound bites, similar to what studios do with movies.

For example, after I spoke at the Gathering, Ted Dekker, a best-selling author and sponsor of the event, said:

> People in their twenties and thirties are inundated with messages and entertainment, making them a hard crowd to please. Michael's keynote . . .

> cut through the clutter and beautifully illustrated the power of a superb storyteller. It was the kind of speech audiences hope for but rarely get.

I include the full quote in the sidebar of the Speaking page on my website. Then I use an excerpt in the body copy itself: "The kind of speech audiences hope for but rarely get." If you string several of these together, you create the same effect movie studios create in their marketing materials.

Bottom line: endorsements can make a huge difference in whether or not your product gets noticed by the gatekeepers, trendsetters, and your target market. Take the time to get them. It is worth it.

FIFTEEN

Get a Great Head Shot

As you build your own platform, you will need photos of yourself. Why? Because people want to connect with people, not merely brands, products, or causes.

The right photo can help establish credibility, build trust, and promote engagement. These are at the heart of connecting in the world of social media and essential if you ever hope to sell someone on what you have to offer.

The key is in getting the right head shot. This is not about creating a Photoshopped glamour photo. It is about capturing the real, authentic you—just as the people who know you best experience you.

So how do you get a head shot for your product, website, or other marketing materials? Here are nine suggestions.

1. **Hire a professional.** Don't simply ask a family member or friend to snap a few quick pictures. And don't settle for some portrait factory. Instead, search the Web for "photography head shot [your city]." Review online portfolios and ask for recommendations from your local camera shop. Expect to pay a few hundred dollars.
2. **Negotiate for all rights.** Make sure you do this on the front end and get it in writing. You don't want to pay a licensing fee every time you use the photo in a different context. Some high-end photographers will not agree to this. If so, keep looking. Photographers are plentiful, and you will readily find one who will work with you.

3. **Don't shoot in a studio.** I know some will disagree with this, but few things look more sterile than a studio. Instead, shoot the photos on your turf, in familiar surroundings. This is so much more interesting and adds more of your personality to the final result.
4. **Wear something appropriate.** The focus should be on your face, not your clothes. By *appropriate,* I mean something neither dated nor too trendy. I always ask myself, *What can I wear that I won't be embarrassed by ten years from now?* You might even want to make a few wardrobe changes during the shoot.
5. **Take lots of photos.** You are not looking for a posed photo. You want something more natural, where your personality is fully expressed. The more photos you take, the more likely you will find ones that work. A good photographer can take a couple of hundred photos (sometimes more) in an hour.
6. **Look into the lens.** You want to make a personal connection. This is really no different than meeting people for the first time—*look directly into their eyes.* The eyes truly are "the window to the soul." One exception is photos of you speaking or performing. However, these aren't technically head shots.
7. **Smile—with your whole face.** I'm not talking about one of those big, cheesy smiles you force yourself to hold about two seconds longer than you are comfortable. I'm talking about a natural smile with your mouth *and your eyes.* (Physiologists sometimes refer to this as the Duchenne smile.[1]) You want to look likable. This is more important than looking professional—whatever that is.
8. **Crop the photo tightly.** We don't need to see your whole body or even your upper torso. We want to focus on your face. While you're at it, ask the photographer to blur the background slightly (photographers call this *bokeh*). This will emphasize your face even more.
9. **Pick one main photo.** Use this on your products, on your website, and as an avatar on all your social media profiles. You want a consistent brand impression. You can also pick a few alternatives, so that your strategic

partners have a few options. I do this on a special promotional materials page of my website. When someone needs a photo, I direct him there.

These are not absolute rules; they are merely suggestions. You can violate them so long as you are doing it for a specific purpose.

Finally, it is a good idea to get your head shots redone every few years. Nothing is quite as jarring as meeting someone who looks ten years older than his photograph—and it could create mistrust where none existed.

SIXTEEN

Develop an Online Media Kit

Once you have completed your work on a new product—whether it is a book, a record, a new CD series, or even a blog—you will probably have some time before it is available to the market. This is the perfect opportunity to get your ducks in a row and prepare for the launch.

One of the first things you need to create is a great online media kit. This is a page on your website or blog where you will want to send strategic partners, media producers, product reviewers, event planners, public relations people, superfans, and anyone else who might want to talk about you or your product. Make it easy! Your media kit is a resource page designed to equip people with all the tools they need to help you get the word out. (It can also help you control your message.)

Include the following eight components. You can alternatively split some of these into separate pages. I'll provide some examples at the end of this chapter.

1. **Headline**. Make it clear what this page is. It might be as simple as the name of your product and the words *Media Kit*.
2. **Navigation**. Provide a table of contents. This provides an overview of the page and a quick way for your visitor to navigate to the parts of the page that are most relevant to him or her. For example, I did this on my Speaking page.[1] Though it's not a media kit per se, it will give you the idea.

3. **Contact Information**. Make it easy on the media, event planners, and your fans. This is often all they are looking for. Put it near the top. Tell people who to contact for inquiries from the media; event or booking inquiries; review copy requests (for books); questions from fans; and all other inquiries.

   If you are going to provide an e-mail address, use a link and encode it, so you don't attract a lot of spam. Also provide links to your social media profiles, including Twitter, Facebook, LinkedIn, Google+, and others.

4. **Product Information**. Provide all the basic product information in one place. Don't make your readers hunt.

   - *Sales copy*. Provide both short (one hundred words or so) and long versions (three to five hundred words) of your sales copy. Bloomberg Media's short version says, "The global business elite relies on Bloomberg more than any other news source." The long form:

     > Bloomberg is a trusted, indispensable source of news and analysis for the largest, most powerful network of global business executives. We've leveraged the innovation and scale of Bloomberg technology, analytics, news and distribution to create an unparalleled, full media spectrum. With 2,300 media professionals in 146 bureaus across 72 countries, we deliver award-winning intelligence, as news happens, from where it happens.[2]

   - *Product specs*. List the simple product or technical specs. For example, for a Coleman Sundome® 4 tent,[3] this would include:

     Weight: 10.2 lbs
     Floor: Polyethylene 1000D-140g/sqm floor
     Limited 1 year warranty
     Made in China

- *Product formats.* List and link any additional product formats the product might be available in, as well as any ancillary products: premium editions, signed editions, DVD study materials, merchandise, workbooks, seminars, conferences, and so forth. This could be anything organically related to the primary product.

  For the Coleman tent above, ancillary products would include a Tent Repair Kit, the CPX™ 6 Lighted Tent Fan, and the CPX™ 4.5 LED Tent Light, as well as the Sundome 2, Sundome 3, Sundome 6, and Elite Sundome 6 tents.[4]

- *Product photos.* Provide more than one photo, preferably from different angles and in 3-D. I use a program called Box Shot 3D.[5] It is powerful and enables me to create product shots like this:

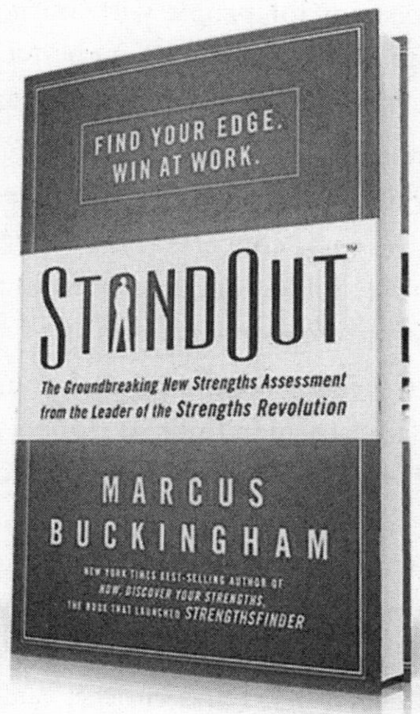

- *Product trailers.* First there were movie trailers. Then there were music videos. Now there are great trailers for speakers, product demos, books, and more. In fact, some people produce more than one. Make sure they are uploaded to a site like Vimeo[6] (my personal preference) or YouTube so people reading the page can embed them on their own site or blog.
- *Full bio.* Provide a short version (one hundred words) and a longer one (three to five hundred words). Don't make this look like a résumé. You only need to include what is relevant to this page's audience.
- *Head shots.* Provide several head shots of yourself, in several sizes. I provide formal, casual, and action shots.
- *Product endorsements.* This is where you include all the celebrity endorsements. Try to get authority figures in your category. If you can't, shoot for people with impressive credentials. If you can't, customer endorsements are better than nothing. See chapter 14 for how to obtain great endorsements.

5. **Promotion Information.** Most readers won't be interested in every aspect of your marketing strategy. However, your live appearances (e.g., speaking events, concerts, presentations) and media appearances (e.g., radio, television, live online chat, blog tour) will be relevant to both professionals and fans.
    - *Live appearances.* Provide a list of your upcoming speaking or concert dates. Include links so readers can get additional information. Here's an excellent example from Ken Davis's site:[7]

> Best-selling author, frequent radio and television guest, and one of the country's most sought after inspirational and motivational speakers—Ken's mixture of side-splitting humor and inspiration delights and enriches audiences of all ages. His books have received national critical acclaim, including the "Book of the Year" award and the Gold Medallion Award. The video and audiotapes of his live appearances are in constant demand.

Ken has been the keynote speaker for hundreds of major corporate events. He is a featured speaker for Promise Keepers and a frequent guest on "Focus on the Family." Ken has made thousands of personal appearances around the world. As president of Dynamic Communicators International, he teaches speaking skills to ministry professionals and corporate executives. Ken's daily radio show, Lighten Up!, is heard on over 1500 stations in the United States and around the world.

February 24th	**Moses Lake, WA / Moses Lake Assembly of God**	**Buy Tickets**
	"Fully Alive" Comedy Concert	
July 19th	**Shipshewana, IN / Blue Gate Theater**	**Buy Tickets**
	A family-friendly night of comedy	
July 26th	**Colorado Springs, CO / Focus on the Family Campus**	**Buy Tickets**
	An educating and equipping conference for families	

- *Media appearances.* Provide a list of your upcoming media appearances so that producers, event planners, and fans can tune in. You might also include highlights from previous appearances.

6. **Interviewer Resources.** You want to make it easy for producers to book you. Provide the following items:
    - *Bio talking points.* This is similar to your bio, but in a talking points format instead of a narrative. This makes it easier for the interviewer to make it sound natural. Here's an example of what I provide to those who introduce me before I speak:[8]

Introduction of Michael Hyatt

Michael Hyatt has spent his career in book publishing. As a publisher, literary agent, and *New York Times* best-selling author, he has a unique perspective on the rapidly changing world of content creation and delivery.

1. **He is currently the chairman of Thomas Nelson Publishers**:
   - The largest faith-based publisher in the world;
   - The oldest commercial publisher still in existence; and
   - The seventh largest trade book publisher in the United States.

He has worked personally with such best-selling authors as Dave Ramsey, John Maxwell, Andy Andrews, and Marcus Buckingham.

2. **Michael is a successful social media practitioner**:
   - His blog, MichaelHyatt.com, is one of the most popular in the world.
   - According to Google, he is ranked in the top 800 of all blogs, with more than 400,000 visitors per month.
   - He typically writes about leadership, personal productivity, and social media.
   - He also has more than 100,000 followers on Twitter.

3. **Most importantly, Michael is a devoted family man**:
   - He has been married to his wife, Gail, for 33 years.
   - They have five daughters, three sons-in-law, and seven grandchildren.
   - He makes his home just outside of Nashville, Tennessee.

He is here [this morning/this afternoon/this evening] to speak to us on the topic of [speech title]. Please join me in welcoming Michael Hyatt.

- *Product summary.* Ninety-five percent of interviewers have probably not used your product or read your book or heard you speak. They're not familiar with your offering. But they want to sound like they are. Summarize it for them. It is an opportunity for you to make the interviewer look smart, which will translate into a good interview and, potentially, more interviews down the road.
- *List of interview topics and angles.* Again, in the spirit of making it easy for producers to book you, provide a list of interview topics and angles. Make them relevant to what people are already talking about. This is one section you will likely need to update as the current news changes.
- *Sample interview questions.* This is the single most important thing you can do to get more, high-quality interviews. Develop a list of seven to ten interview questions. This allows both you and the interviewer to look smart.

7. **Fan Resources**. It's great to have fans. It is even better to turn fans into evangelists. But in order to do this, you have to equip them to work on your behalf.

    - *Samples.* Give your fans something to share with others. Sample quotes from your seminar, light versions of your app, or sample chapters from your book. One great tool for authors is Scribd.[9] Why? Because your fans can embed the sample chapters in their own blog to share it with others.
    - *Twitter post samples.* Make it easy. Give your followers ten to thirty sample tweets. Suggest a hashtag so you can track all the tweets in one place. (See chapter 43, "Understand Twitter Basics.")
    - *Banner ads.* Commission the design of banner ads that your fans can put on their own blogs or websites. These are cheaper than you think. Just search Google for "cheap banner ad design." You should create ads for all the standard banner ad sizes.
    - *Incentives.* Give people an opportunity to connect with you based on how many of your products they buy or what they are willing to do to promote them. Gary Vaynerchuck and Phil Cooke are two examples of this.

Vaynerchuck offers a *Crush It!* wristband if you buy three books, a personalized video from Gary for buying fifty books, and an hour of one-on-one Skype time with him for buying three hundred books. If you buy one thousand books, you'll receive dinner with Gary in New York City.[10] Cooke had similar deals for his book *Jolt!*[11]

Be creative!

- *Wallpaper*. Some of your fans want "digital bling." They will proudly display it on their computer. What can be more personal than that? A good designer can crank out wallpaper using your exiting graphics in less than thirty minutes.
- *Merchandise*. Some of your fans want "physical bling." They identify with your brand or your product so much that they are willing to wear it, display it, or drink from it.[12]

8. **Media Reactions.** This is basically a "wall of fame." Include your best product reviews, customer reviews, Twitter comments, Facebook comments, Google+ comments, and so on. The idea here is to share endorsements and enthusiasm from your fans to fuel even more enthusiasm.

The best example of a media kit I have ever seen is the most recent one for Andy Andrews's book *The Final Summit*. [13] It meets nearly all my criteria. Make sure you download the PDF as well.[14]

Also, check out the online media kits for Dave Ramsey's book *EntreLeadership*,[15] Dov Seldman's book *How: Why How We Do Anything Means Everything*,[16] and Jenny Blake's book *Life After College*.[17]

If you want to equip your potential partners and fans to get the word out, take the time to build a great online media kit.

We've covered a lot in this section. From defining your goals to assembling your pit crew to securing raving endorsements, you've learned about the need to do your prep work well. Done with care and intent, these will become the footings, posts, beams, and joists for your platform.

In the next section we'll begin building on that solid substructure as we cover the important elements to building your social media home base.

PART THREE

BUILD YOUR HOME BASE

SEVENTEEN

Understand the Model

Let's talk about adding the planks to your platform, creating a home base that is solid and provides strong footing to grow from. Planks include everything from Facebook, Twitter, your blog, your website, even traditional media. And learning how to weave all of these things seamlessly is an art unto itself.

These days I find myself increasingly speaking on the topic of social media, because I am a blogger who has fed the growth of my blog's audience—and, therefore, the size of my platform—through social media, primarily Facebook and Twitter.

I am often asked how it all functions together. People say, "Okay, I get the website and the blog thing. I understand Facebook and Twitter—sort of. But how does it all fit?"

Some time ago I heard Chris Brogan (coauthor of *Trust Agents*[1] and a columnist with *Entrepreneur* magazine) lecture in New York on social media. He introduced the concept of a "simple presence framework." Several months later, Jon Dale, a consultant to Thomas Nelson, where I was CEO at the time, introduced us to a similar concept. He called it a "social media framework."[2]

Here is my version. (I have borrowed concepts and terms from both—and others—but this is my particular recipe. I would encourage you to read theirs as well.)

A good social media strategy has three components.

1. **A Home Base.** This is a digital property you own and control. It is where your loyal fans gather. It can be as simple as a blog or a website or as complex as a self-hosted community. Regardless, it is where you direct all Internet traffic. Why? Because this is the place where you can best sell your ideas or products. You control the borders and determine who has access.
2. **Embassies.** These are places you don't own, but where you have a registered profile. In other words, you have a regular presence on someone else's property. You engage in conversations with those who congregate there. Examples include Facebook, Twitter, LinkedIn, or even other blogs you follow. You generally need a "passport" (verified credentials) granted by the site owner to maintain residency or participate in conversations.
3. **Outposts.** These are places you don't own nor do you have a regular presence. Instead, you simply listen into conversations about you, your brand, your company, or topics that interest you. For example, I have search columns in HootSuite[3] that monitor mentions of both my name and my company. I also use Google Alerts[4] to monitor the same information wherever it may occur on the Web.

The bottom line is that all the social media tools available fit into one of these three buckets. If you are just involved in social media for the sake of entertainment, you may not need a home base. But if you are serious about building a platform, that's precisely where you need to start. From there you can set up embassies and outposts.

EIGHTEEN

Focus Your Efforts Online

The most effective way to sell anything is word of mouth. Consumers trust the recommendations of their family, friends, and coworkers. They have credibility that you can never hope to have.

This begs the question, "How do you get word of mouth started?"

Certainly it begins by creating a great product or service—something truly wow, as we discussed in part 1. And that's why advertising guru David Ogilvy's statement "Great marketing only makes a bad product fail faster" is so apt, because word of mouth actually works against a disappointing product.

Once you have a great product, you have to get the word out. At that point it becomes a question of how to spread your message in the most cost-effective manner.

Certainly you can use commercial mass media, including TV, radio, print ads, billboards, and so on. But, generally speaking, this is a waste of money. Only a narrow subset of the audience you are paying to reach could be viewed as (a) potential customers of your product or service, and (b) people who know your brand. Worse, more than ever, many studies reveal that people distrust advertising, so the message is suspect from the get-go. It takes enormous frequency to overcome this—something that most project budgets can't justify.

This is why I oppose almost all one-off magazine or newspaper ads. Instead, it's better to "narrowcast" the message to a target audience. There is no cheaper way to do this than on the Internet, where you can build a tribe of followers that eagerly anticipates your next communiqué.

This is all more or less common sense. The problem is that the Internet per se is not enough. You can't just hang a website in cyberspace and expect its mere presence to create a following. If you build it, they may not come. It's like putting up a billboard in the desert ten miles from the nearest road.

When I was a publisher at Thomas Nelson in the early 2000s, we went website crazy. We had a corporate site, of course. In the rush to take advantage of the Internet, each of our divisions also built a site. Then we started building sites for individual authors. Finally, we began building individual sites for each of our books. We naively thought this was marketing.

This was before blogging really came into being. These were *static* sites. We built them and then never really updated them. You can guess what happened: nothing.

We literally built over one thousand sites and none of them got any meaningful traffic. It was like printing a beautiful brochure, sticking them in your warehouse, and then wondering why people aren't buying your products. What we learned is that for an online strategy to work, you need to create a site that makes people want to come back for more—and bring a few of their friends with them. The problem was not with online marketing; the problem was the way we were using it.

This is when I began to experiment with my own blog. I noticed that if I updated my content frequently, people would come back. If I wrote really compelling content, people would tell their friends.

From there, we began to experiment with some of our authors. They began blogging and used it as the foundation of their own platforms. It paid big dividends for many. That's why today I am a strong proponent of focusing your efforts online. It offers the best return for the investment. In the rest of this section we'll discuss how to take advantage of online tools to build your own platform.

By the way, this is not an either/or proposition—offline or online. I believe in both. What I am suggesting is that most people can build an online platform easier and cheaper than any other way.

NINETEEN

Beware of Self-Proclaimed Social Media Experts

If building your brand or platform is starting to sound too complicated or time-consuming, and you're thinking about hiring someone to do it all for you, please consider this warning: not everyone has the expertise they claim.

For example, I am increasingly being pitched by so-called social media experts. A very few are bona fide experts. Some are traditional media people who are repacking the same old advice using the new buzzwords. More than a few are unemployed marketing people who discovered Twitter last month. In fact, I checked out one recently who had no blog and only a few hundred Twitter followers. There's no crime in that, of course . . . unless you are billing yourself as a social media expert. Then it's just ludicrous.

How do you tell the difference? Here are three rules:

1. Make sure the expert's claims are backed up by his numbers.
2. Make sure he has been where you want to go.
3. Make sure he knows how to replicate his success.

You wouldn't want to attempt to climb Mount Everest, get halfway up the mountain, and then discover this is your guide's first climb. Neither do you want to follow the advice of someone who is (as they say in Texas) "all hat and no cattle." Reading a few books and articles on social media is not the same as building a successful social media platform.

Rather than walking you through some negative examples, let me give you some positive ones. I faithfully read the blogs of Seth Godin, Chris Brogan, and Tim Ferriss.[1] I would be happy to take advice from any of them on building blog traffic.

Why? I checked the numbers from Compete.com.[2] (Caveat: this tool is not one hundred percent accurate, but it is close enough for double-checking someone's claims.)

They all have more traffic than I do. Therefore, when they speak, I listen.

Or take Twitter. I get pitched several times a day from people who know "how to dramatically grow your follower count on Twitter." This claim to expertise is easy to check as well. In fact, if the so-called expert doesn't have more traffic than I do, I ignore him. On the other hand, the last I checked, Guy Kawasaki has over 450,000 followers,[3] Chris Brogan has more than 200,000,[4] and Tim Ferriss has 300,000-plus.[5] (Seth Godin is not personally on Twitter as of this writing.)

Again, I would be happy to take advice from them because they have built large followings—without the benefit of traditional media platforms (e.g., a television show, movie career, career in politics). Unfortunately, most of the people who are out there touting themselves as social media experts aren't. It's up to you to know the difference. That's why you should start with the numbers.

TWENTY

Start a Blog (or Restart One)

For many of us, the heart of our home base is our blog. It's where our best thinking lives, the place where others can comment and interact with us, the nexus of our social network. In the years I've been writing my blog, several readers have contacted me, asking how to get started. Believe it or not, the process is easier than you may think.

Here are eight steps:

1. **Determine a theme.** I'm not talking about your design theme, but your content. Most bloggers take one of three approaches. Some write on whatever happens to interest them at the moment. In this sense, their blogs are truly "web journals." Others select a single theme and stick to it. Frankly, this takes a lot of discipline. Still others, like me, focus on a primary theme but occasionally deviate from it. If you want to develop a following of loyal readers, I think the latter two approaches are best. People who have similar interests will keep coming back for more.

   Before you begin, ask yourself these two vital questions:

   - Can you generate high-quality content on a regular basis? (And by "regular," I mean at least three times a week.)
   - Will your content attract a loyal and growing audience? This might not be your goal, but you won't generate enough income to cover your costs unless you do. (More on monetizing your blog in a later chapter.)

I am not trying to discourage you. Honestly. But don't invest a bunch of time and money until you can answer these questions with a resounding yes. The truth is, most people who start a blog quit within a few months. (Reread that sentence and let it sink in.)

2. **Select a service**. I use WordPress.org (the self-hosted version).[1] However, there are scores of services available. If you are just starting out, I recommend—in my order of preference—WordPress.com (the hosted version), TypePad.com, or Blogger.com. If you attain some success and want the ability to customize nearly everything, I recommend WordPress.org. At that point, you will have to select a hosting service and then install WordPress on it.

   While the basic, self-hosted version of WordPress is free, it is like a crack cocaine sample. It is designed to get you hooked. Once you migrate to WordPress.org, the expenses begin to mount.

   I spend more than a thousand dollars a month on my blog. I know this is shocking to most people. This amount includes hosting, server administration, custom programming, software services, troubleshooting, and more. Sometimes I feel like it is a black hole.

   Yet for me it is worth it because of the traffic I generate and the income it produces from ads, affiliate commissions, and product sales. Nonetheless it has taken me years to get to this place. And it is not the place to start.

   That's why I recommend starting with WordPress.com. You can get up and running quickly.

3. **Set up your blog**. Most of the blogging services I have looked at make this a very simple process. Don't be put off because it sounds technical. It usually isn't. You won't need to become a geek. However, you will have to make some decisions about how you want your blog to look.

   For example, you'll have to decide on a theme. In this context, that means the colors, number of columns, and the overall look and feel of your blog. You will likely want to include your picture. If so, you'll need a digital copy. Regardless, this is something you can tweak as you go.

4. **Write your first post.** If you haven't done a lot of writing, this may prove to be the most difficult part. Keep your posts short if you don't have a lot of experience. (I recommend less than five hundred words.) Develop momentum. Get the hang of it. Stick to what you know.

You probably take for granted the fact that you have a great deal of specialized information that others will find helpful—possibly even fascinating. If you don't know where else to start, begin with a "Welcome to My Blog" post. Tell your prospective readers why you have started your blog and what kinds of things you intend to write about. Here's my first blog posting, which was written to the employees at Thomas Nelson Publishers when I was the CEO.

WELCOME TO MY NEW BLOG!—MARCH 29, 2005

I have been trying to figure out some way to communicate with our employees on some sort of regular basis. I considered a "Webcast." In fact, we even videotaped one. But, frankly, it looked forced and artificial. We ended up scuttling the project.

I also considered sending out a semiregular e-mail blast. This certainly has its advantages. For starters, I can communicate to almost every employee without any initiative on their part. In addition, it's free.

However, after thinking about it for a few weeks and after consulting with a few of our executives, I decided to set up a blog (short for "Web Log"). That's what you are reading now.

I think it has several advantages:

1. **It is a familiar medium**. It's different than a book or a newsletter, to be sure, but it is still publishing. As a company, this is a medium we understand. Also, as a writer myself, it's a medium I understand, which is important if I'm going to do this on a regular basis. I have been writing another blog for several months and have enjoyed the process. It allows me to

write whenever I want without the expectation that it has to be at regular intervals.

2. **It provides a mechanism for feedback**. E-mail does this, too, of course. All you have to do is "Reply." However, it excludes other people from the conversation unless you "Reply All." Unfortunately, that would generate hundreds of e-mail messages since I would be sending the original e-mail to more than 600 employees. By contrast, this blog allows for comments (see the bottom of this post). You can even enter your comments anonymously if you wish.
3. **It provides an archive of communications**. This feature allows you to catch up if you have missed some of my posts. I think it might also prove helpful to new employees, allowing them to read the entries that interest them whenever they have the opportunity or interest.
4. **It may encourage you to start your own blog**. I have been hoping that we would have several employees start blogging. Many companies are now doing this, including Microsoft. They have over 1,000 employees blogging. This is a great way to encourage communication within the company. It is also a great way to let the outside world know what goes on inside a company like ours. It can also be a low-key way to promote our company and our products.
5. **It is inexpensive**. TypePad, the blogging service I use, charges just $4.95 a month. It's hard to beat that. If you are interested in writing your own blog, TypePad offers a thirty-day free trial.

Here's how I anticipate this working. Periodically, I will write a new post. It might be several per week or one a month. I honestly can't predict the frequency. Regardless, I will send out an e-mail to everyone when I do, alerting you that a new entry has been posted. From there, it's up to you.

Please do provide me with feedback. I want to hear "the good, the bad, and the ugly." If you disagree with me or want to provide an alternative perspective, go for it! If you are uncomfortable using your real name, use an alias. The important thing is to tell me what's on your mind.

5. **Consider using an off-line blogging client.** This isn't a necessity, but it will make blogging much easier. An off-line blogging client is like a word processor for blogging. It enables you to write when you're not online and then upload your post when you connect to the Internet. You can also schedule posts to run on a specific day and time, which is a very useful function when your schedule is tight or you'd like to take a vacation. The two most popular are BlogJet[2] (for Windows) and MarsEdit[3] (for Mac). When I switched to MarsEdit, I never looked back.
6. **Add the bells and whistles.** Most blogs allow you to post the books you are reading, albums you enjoy, and various other lists. TypePad[4] is especially adept at this. You can also incorporate third-party services like MailChimp,[5] AWeber,[6] FeedBlitz,[7] or FeedBurner.[8] These enable your readers to subscribe to your site and even receive an e-mail whenever you post a new entry. The best way to get an idea of what is available is to read other people's blogs and take note of what you like.
7. **Publicize your blog.** You'll want to make sure you're "pinging" the major weblog tracking sites. Most of the blogging services handle this automatically, as do the off-line blogging clients. Don't worry if you don't understand this process. You don't need to understand it to use it. Here's a simple explanation.

   Usually your service or software will send a notification to the tracking sites to alert them that you have posted a new entry. If your software doesn't allow this, you might want to make use of Ping-o-matic.[9] This is a super easy service that will ping eighteen different services. All you have to do is enter your blog address whenever you post a new entry.

8. **Write regularly.** This is the best advice I could give you for building readership. If people like what you write, they will come back. If there's nothing new to read, they will eventually lose interest. So the more regularly you post, the more your readership will grow. I suggest you schedule time to write. It won't happen on its own.

   Setting up a blog is the easy part; actual blogging is the hard part. Once the initial enthusiasm wanes, it is difficult to keep posting. Most would-be bloggers post less and less until they simply quit and abandon their blogs. At some point, it comes down to making a commitment and sticking to it.

Finally, I would suggest that you be patient with yourself. Writing is like anything else. The more you do it, the better you get. If you have a little talent and stick with it, you'll eventually get into the rhythm and joy of it.

While Facebook and Twitter can be effective in driving people to your blog, it is your blog itself with which you will primarily build your platform. Take it seriously, and it will serve you well!

TWENTY-ONE

Create the Content Yourself

A few years ago, I taught a seminar on blogging at a trade show. The CEO from one of the largest companies at the trade show attended. Afterward he came up and introduced himself. He asked if we could have breakfast the next morning. "Sure," I said.

So the next morning we met. He asked, "How do I get started blogging?" My heart leapt. I knew he would have an instant audience. I, for one, would love to read what he had to say. I imagined all kinds of things I could learn from him.

Then he dashed my hopes. "Who ghostwrites your blog?" he asked.

"Excuse me?" I choked.

"I mean, who do you use to write your blog? Could I possibly hire him or could you recommend someone who is really good?"

Honestly, I couldn't believe what I was hearing. The guy obviously did not get it. I blurted out, "I don't use a ghostwriter. I write every word myself."

"Oh, I couldn't possibly do that," he said. "I don't have the time."

Without thinking, I said, "Then you shouldn't do it at all."

I still feel that way. You can hire a ghostwriter to write a book. You might even be able to hire someone to write an occasional op-ed piece or magazine article. Usually, no one will even know unless you choose to reveal it.

But this is not true with blogs. It is especially not true with Twitter. If you try, you will be found out. Your readers will know. You will be considered a "poser," someone pretending to be something he is not. And trust me, word will spread. In the end, you will do irreparable damage to your personal brand.

I have seen this trend of ghost-blogging and ghost-tweeting with authors, artists, and other celebrities. Forget the fact that blogging is more than a decade old and Twitter is already a mature medium. Now that these and other social media have gone mainstream, no one wants to be left behind. Everyone is jumping on board.

What some of these new converts don't understand is that social media only works well if the communication is personal, authentic, and near immediate. Here's what I mean:

1. **Personal**. Even if people don't know you, they can tell if you are the one writing. You might be able to fool them for a while, but blogging and tweeting require you to express your personality. If you don't, readers sense that something is not quite right.
2. **Authentic**. People will only trust you if you are willing to pull back the curtain of your life and give them a peek inside. Of course, this is helpful in every form of communication. It connects people in a powerful way. But it is essential with blogging and tweeting. You must be willing to share yourself.
3. **Immediate.** Blogging and tweeting are a dialogue. You get to introduce the topic and may even moderate it, but you are expected to participate in the ongoing conversation. As a result, you must respond to some blog comments and most Twitter replies and direct messages.

All of this requires your personal participation. You can't hire it done. You can't fake it. If you're not willing to make the personal investment, don't bother. You won't fool anyone.

TWENTY-TWO

Use a Blog Post Template

People often ask me if I use some sort of template when I write one of my typical five-hundred word posts. The answer is yes.

I do, in fact, use a blog post template. A blog post template is nothing more than a generic outline that I follow for most posts. I don't follow it slavishly, but I always start with it. It includes all the elements that I have learned make for an effective post. It also helps me write faster, because it provides me with a track to run on.

My blog post template consists of five components:

1. **Lead Paragraph**. This is key. If you take too long on the windup, you will lose readers. You have to get into the premise of the post and make it relevant to your readers. After the title, this is the second most important component of your post.
2. **Relevant Image**. Bloggers should use images for the same reasons magazines do: you want to pull readers into the post itself. Pictures do that. I get 90 percent of mine from iStockPhoto.com.[1] Occasionally I use a screenshot or an embedded video or slideshow.
3. **Personal Experience**. I always try to share a personal experience. The more honest and transparent you can be, the better. Why? Because readers connect with stories. In fact, my most popular posts generally come out of my stories about some failure on my part.
4. **Main Body**. Everything to this point has been an introduction. Try to make the main content scannable. I use bullets, numbered lists—and

often both. This makes the content more accessible to readers and more sharable via Twitter and Facebook.

5. **Discussion Question**. For the past few years, I have ended every post with a question. I don't intend my posts to be a monologue. Instead, I want to start a conversation. As a result, I measure my effectiveness at this by how many comments I get.

I also follow a few overall rules when writing my posts:

- **Make the posts short**. Aim for five hundred words. For those of us who tend to be too thorough, this usually means you'll have to write the post and then go back and tighten it up.
- **Use short paragraphs**. Try to stick to three to four sentences per paragraph. If it's more than this, the content looks too dense. Readers will give up and move on. (Notice how newspapers usually follow this rule.)
- **Keep sentences short**. As a general rule, try to avoid compound sentences. A period gives readers a natural stop—and a sense of progress as they pass one milestone after another. To quote a common copywriting axiom, short sentences make the copy "read fast."
- **Use simple words.** I love language, so I am often tempted to use big words. Nonetheless, I have learned to avoid this. The goal is to communicate, not to impress readers with your vocabulary.
- **Provide internal links.** You can't say everything in one post, so link to other posts where you have developed a thought in more detail. This has the added advantage of increasing your page views and session times. I think it is also genuinely helpful to readers.

While your template might be different, it is worth outlining and tweaking as you hone your writing skills. This will allow you to write faster and more effectively.

TWENTY-THREE

Maintain a List of Post Ideas

The dreaded writer's block afflicts us all from time to time. You will eventually struggle with it. Occasionally I have an easy run of several days, when the ideas seem to flow effortlessly. But that is rare—most weeks, I get stuck at least once or twice.

So what can you do? This seems almost too obvious to mention, but you should keep a list of your ideas—the ones that come to you when you don't have time to follow up, like when you're driving to work. I maintain a list in Evernote and refer to it regularly.

But if your idea list is thin, you need idea starters. Here are thirteen of them. I offer these up as possibilities for lighting a fire when your brain is damp. (If you happen to be a novelist, see Appendix B for some specialized advice.)

1. **Tell a personal story**. This almost always works, because you harness the power of your own personal narrative. It is particularly good if it is dramatic and you feel the freedom to be transparent. It is helpful if you can conclude with a lesson or two that you have learned.

   Man of the House, a Proctor and Gamble blog especially for men, has some great examples of this. One of its bloggers, James Pilcher, blogged about telling his family he lost his job. "I'll never forget it as long as I live . . . I was as angry, hurt, scared, and vulnerable as I ever have been." Pilcher went on to give some excellent advice for anyone facing a job loss.[1]

2. **Describe a historical event.** This is very similar to using a personal story. History is full of great stories. It's one of the reasons why I am almost always reading a history book or biography of some kind. Again, you can tell the story and distill the lessons.

   Erin Glover did this quite effectively, for example, when she wrote a blog for the *Disney Parks Blog* highlighting the 1937 premiere of *Snow White and the Seven Dwarfs*. The sold-out opening night took place on December 21 that year at the Carthay Circle Theatre.

   Glover's blog, written the same date seventy-four years later, was flush with historical pictures of the big night, where more than thirty thousand fans gathered outside the theater just to be part of the event. The takeaway from Glover's blog? She was getting the buzz started for the opening of the Carthay Circle Theatre coming the next year at Disney's California Adventure Park.[2]

3. **Review a book, movie, or software program.** This is a great way to share some of the resources you have found and why you liked them. It can also help your readers avoid products or experiences that were not so helpful. What are some of your favorite resources?

4. **Comment on a powerful quote.** I can't read a book without underlining the passages that impress me. Occasionally, I go back and post the quotes that stand alone. Also, from time to time, I post the quote and comment on why a particular quote was meaningful.

5. **Let a great photograph inspire you.** Behind every great photo is a story. You may know the story or you may not. Regardless, you can find one in the photo. Some of the best ones are posted on Flickr.com.[3] You can use these in accordance with a Creative Commons License.[4]

6. **Comment on something in the news.** This can be something global or something that is specific to your industry. If you are a thought leader—or trying to establish yourself as a thought leader—this is a great way to do that.

7. **Report on an interesting conversation.** I meet lots of interesting people. I'll bet you do too. Some of them I meet at work; some of them I meet in my social life. Regardless, rarely a week goes by that I am

not deeply stimulated by a conversation I have had. Why not blog on that? Be careful that you don't reveal something you shouldn't. In order to protect the privacy of others, you might want to change the names or alter the circumstances slightly.

8. **Provide a step-by-step explanation for how to do something.** When you provide five steps to this, or four strategies for that, people gobble it up. I think all of us have a need for down-to-earth, practical help with the items that interest us.
9. **Provide a list of resources.** This is a huge way to give back to your industry or community. It is easy to take for granted what you know. You are probably sitting on priceless information that others would die to have access to. Resource lists are a great way to build traffic.
10. **Answer your readers' questions.** My readers ask some of the best questions. Sometimes they e-mail them. Sometimes they put them in the comments of an older post. Often they just tweet them to me. I assume that if one person has the question, so do others. By answering these, you demonstrate that you are listening.
11. **Make a seemingly overwhelming task simple.** There is a huge audience for anyone who can make complex things simple. Provide a conceptual model, an outline, or an introduction to something you take for granted.
12. **Explain the rationale behind a decision.** Intelligent people want to know why you do what you do. That is what makes everyone so interesting. You can explain the rationale behind almost any decision you have made, and it will be instructive for others.
13. **Write a guide to something popular.** This is especially good for technology topics—anything in which people feel overwhelmed. I have written introductions to social networking, how to stay on top of e-mail, and how to create a life plan. The key is to assume the reader knows nothing about the topic.

Next time you get stuck, you might want to review your idea list and these suggestions. Sometimes, all it takes is a spark to reignite the fire.

TWENTY-FOUR

Write Posts Faster

If you are like most bloggers, you are trying to squeeze writing your posts in between your job, your family, and a thousand other activities. It can be really tough to be consistent.

After writing more than twelve hundred posts, I have gotten better and faster with practice. Now, on average, it takes me sixty to seventy minutes to write and format a single post. I thought I would share eleven of the tricks I use to write more efficiently.

1. **Start the night before.** Research from the University of California–San Diego School of Medicine shows that Rapid Eye Movement (REM) sleep directly enhances creative processing more than any other sleep or wake state.[1]

   Put this information to good use by sleeping on your blogging thoughts. I try to determine what I am going to write about the next day before I go to bed. This allows my mind to begin engaging with the topic in advance. It's like putting a roast in a Crock-Pot and letting it simmer overnight.

2. **Use downtime to think.** Downtime does not mean you are doing nothing. On the contrary. You can work "think time" into many of your normal, active routines. For example, I run or work out for sixty minutes almost every morning. During this time, I listen to an audio book for thirty minutes. This often provides raw material for future posts. Then I turn it off and just think. I primarily focus on what I

am going to blog about that day. I usually create my main premise and outline in my head. Try using downtime during your next commute to think, and it will make your drive time a valuable asset.

3. **Go off-line**. When it is time to write, go off-line. You can't be completely off-line, because you need to be able to use the Web for research. But you don't need to be checking e-mail, Twitter, or Facebook. Enter Anti-Social.[2] This little program enables you to turn off e-mail and all your social networks. You can't get back to them without rebooting your computer. If you are a PC user, Cold Turkey[3] is similar.
4. **Turn on some music**. Years ago, I discovered that certain kinds of music put me in my zone. I have a playlist of music in iTunes I call "Background Music for Writing." It consists mostly of soundtracks from movies like *The Bucket List*, *Seabiscuit*, and *The Horse Whisperer*. I also occasionally listen to Lifescapes Music.[4]
5. **Set a timer**. If you are naturally competitive with yourself or others, use it to your advantage. Help yourself get started and avoid distractions by setting a timer for seventy minutes. It creates a sense of urgency. I am very competitive with myself, and I find myself engaging immediately and racing the clock to finish.
6. **Use a template**. As I discussed in a previous chapter, this helps too. I use a formula based on the SCORRE method taught by Ken Davis at the SCORRE Conference.[5] (If you haven't attended this conference, put it on your bucket list. It's one of the best things I have ever done professionally.) I start with an Evernote template and then actually do the writing in ByWord,[6] a stripped-down word processor.
7. **Create an outline**. In case you haven't noticed, I like lists. Lists make posts highly scannable, which also makes them easier for readers to digest. It also makes them easier to write. If you know the overview before you begin, it almost becomes an exercise in fill-in-the-blank.
8. **Write without editing**. Don't try to write and edit at the same time. If you do, you will drive yourself crazy. Worse, you won't make much progress. Writing is primarily a right-brain function. Editing is a left-brain function. Switching back and forth between these two

hemispheres slows you down. You don't really get into the groove like you should. Instead, just write continuously without stopping.

9. **Now edit and format.** Once you have a first draft, begin the editing process. Read back through your post a few times, cleaning up the spelling, grammar, and syntax. Also try to shorten everything you can. Use simple words, short sentences, and short paragraphs. This is one of the most important things you can do to make your posts read faster.
10. **Add graphics, links, and metadata.** Once I am happy with my post, I copy and paste everything from ByWord to MarsEdit.[7] (This is my off-line blogging software.) There I add graphics, usually a single photo from iStockPhoto.com.[8] In addition, I add internal and external links and the all-important metadata (e.g., category, post description, keywords).
11. **Publish a draft.** Once I am done, I set the publication date and time in MarsEdit and publish the post. Technically, this creates a scheduled post. It won't be live on my site until the appointed date and time. Now I go into my WordPress admin panel and run the post through Scribe,[9] a program that analyzes my content and offers suggestions on making it more search engine friendly. Once I am happy with the score (I always shoot for 100 percent), I update the post. I'm done!

Sometimes it takes a little longer than seventy minutes. Sometimes it takes less. But I find that I get more written when I focus on these short deadlines than when I don't. This sense of progress encourages me to write more.

TWENTY-FIVE

Create Video Interviews

Videos are a quick way to keep your readers engaged with your blog. As a book publisher, I have posted video interviews with authors, including Todd Burpo, Guy Kawasaki, and Scott Schwertly. I think this is more interesting than simply reading a written review. Both have their place, but a video interview provides a unique perspective on the book from the author's vantage point.

More recently I posted a video on how to use Google Reader to keep up with your favorite blogs. Sometimes it's much more effective to show than tell.[1] I watch a lot of how-to videos when I am trying to learn something.

Video interviews are super easy to do. You can record the video, do the editing, and write the post in an hour or less (not including the time you spend prepping for what you're going to talk about). It is a very efficient use of your time.

Here are the steps I typically go through to interview someone. For other types of videos, pick it up at step 6:

1. **Schedule the video interview.** Ask the person you are interviewing to block thirty minutes for the call. (If everything is working on both ends, you should be done in fifteen minutes.) Confirm that they have Skype installed, and ask for their Skype user name. Then put the call on your calendar and include their Skype user name in the notes.
2. **Prepare for the interview.** This will vary according to what you're taping. Since I am interviewing authors, this means reading their book. I

highlight and mark it as I go. Type out a list of five to seven questions you plan to ask. Then display these questions in a text editor directly under your webcam.

3. **Send the questions to the person you are interviewing.** Some people prefer to respond live, without preparation. Others want to prepare. Regardless, send the questions and anything else needed to help the person be prepared. When I interview authors, for example, after the question I also include a page reference in the book we're discussing—just to make it easy on them. Also confirm the call time.
4. **Call the person using Skype.** Use Call Recorder for Skype[2] to actually record the video and audio. My preference settings, accessed from within the Skype preference panel, are set as follows:

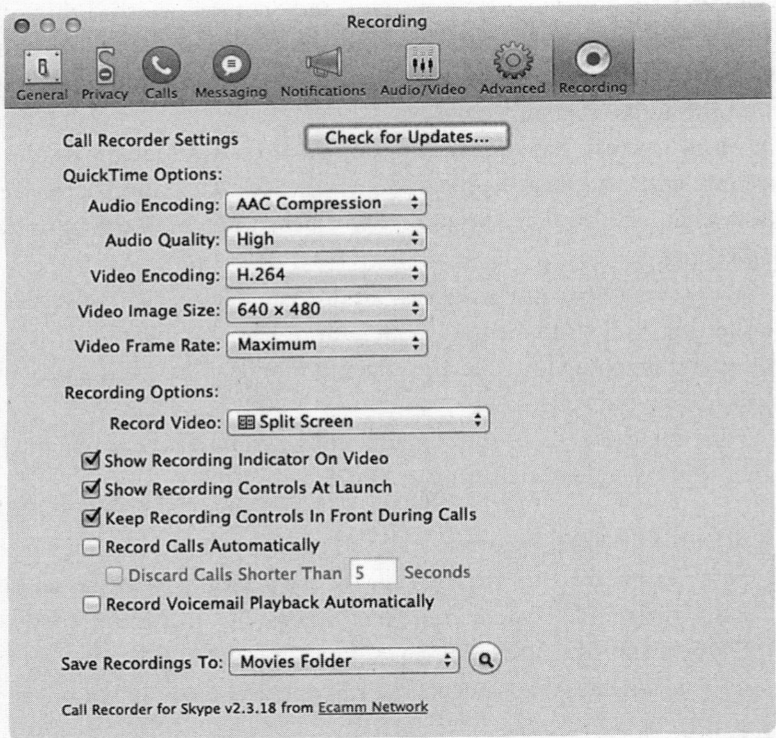

Notice that the Recording Options: Record Video is set to "Split Screen."

5. **Record the video interview.** Make sure you are both ready, and then click the record button on Call Recorder. Try to look into the webcam as much as possible, though you'll be tempted to look at the image of the person you are interviewing. When you are finished, turn the recorder off. The call will be saved in the folder you designated under your preference settings.
6. **Edit the video with your favorite editing program.** You can use something as simple as QuickTime Pro.[3] I use iMovie. I generally don't edit anything within the body of the video itself. I simply trim off the beginning (when we are getting set up) and the end. I also insert a video intro and outro at the beginning and the end. I had these professionally created by Duarte Design.[4] I use a simple cross-fade transition between each element.
7. **Upload to your favorite video-sharing site.** I upload directly to Vimeo from within iMovie. You can also upload to YouTube or even Facebook. Set the video to "Make this movie personal." You will want to double-check it on the YouTube site before going live to the world. (Once you are happy with the metadata and thumbnail, flip the settings on YouTube to "Public.")
8. **Embed a link to the video into your blog.** This will vary, depending on your blogging platform and the software you use to access it. I do mine with a code from within MarsEdit, my blogging software. I have the embed code mapped to a single keystroke. Write a brief post around the video, introducing it. If you recorded an interview, include the questions you asked the person. This will help draw people into the video itself.

In addition to this, send a preview link of the post to the person you interviewed before you go live with it. (I do this with WordPress using a plugin called Public Post Preview.[5] This enables me to give a link to him or her to view the post before it is published.)

All in all, this is a pretty straightforward process. It creates some variety in your content delivery and gives your readers a perspective they might not otherwise get.

TWENTY-SIX

Don't Hire a Proofreader

If you post often, you will inevitably get some e-mails from readers who have caught typos in your blog posts. Most of those who have contacted me go out of their way to apologize for bringing the subject up. Regardless, always be appreciative. I fix the error, thank the reader, and move on.

However, on occasion you will get an e-mail from a self-appointed member of the Grammar Police. He or she feels compelled not only to point out your errors but to chide you.

For example, someone recently wrote this to me:

> You should be ashamed. How can you be a book publisher and allow such embarrassing errors on your blog? I am disappointed by your lack of commitment to excellence. It makes me think less of your company. Please: do us all a favor and hire a proofreader!

I am just grateful I am not married to this person!

Should you hire someone to proofread your blog posts? In my opinion, no. Here's why:

1. **It will delay "shipping."** You can fiddle with your writing until it is perfect (an illusion, by the way), or you can publish and move on to the next thing. Perfectionism is the mother of procrastination.
2. **Blogs are not books.** If you have an error in a book, it is permanent—at least until the next edition. Not so with blogs. You can make corrections on the fly and republish the post immediately.

3. **Even proofreaders don't catch every typo.** Book publishers use multiple proofers on every book as a matter of course. Still, they don't catch everything. Those pesky little errors hide in the shadows and only show up once the book is printed. How much proofing is enough? Most of us can't afford perfection.

I think the better approach is to stay focused on your writing and your output. Churn out the posts. The more you write, the better you will get.

Obviously you will want to read your post several times before you upload it. The following process works well:

- Read through it twice after you have written it.
- Read it once out loud.
- Publish as a draft and read through it on the blog itself.

Some errors will still slip through the cracks. But at some point, it's time to hit the "Publish" button and be done with it.

From there, crowdsource your proofreading. Your regular readers are happy to do it. Spend your time writing content that adds value rather than obsessing over every typo, misspelling, and grammatical error.

TWENTY-SEVEN

Protect Your Intellectual Property

It's inevitable. If you are successful as a blogger, people are going to steal your content, otherwise known as *intellectual property*. That's like someone's trying to steal part of your home base, and it's not a pleasant experience. You'll wake up one morning to a Google Alert notifying you that your name was mentioned on another blog.

Great, you'll think, *I love free publicity. I also know that inbound links help increase my search engine rankings.*

You then click on the link to read the post. To your horror, you discover that another blogger has reposted one of your entire blog posts, word for word.

This has happened to me several times. Each time, it takes my breath away. I feel violated. I think, *I spent a considerable amount of time creating that post, and he just reposted it without my permission?*

What do you do?

First of all, breathe. This is not the end of the world. As a writer, your biggest problem is obscurity, not piracy. The very fact that someone thought enough of your work to repost it on his own blog means he values it. You should first of all take it as a compliment.

There are eight ways you can protect your intellectual property online. If you follow these steps, they will dramatically reduce the chances of your content being stolen. They will also provide a strategy for dealing with it when it happens.

1. **Understand copyright law.** Your post is protected from the moment you create it. You don't have to register it. It is your intellectual property, and no one can legally reproduce it. Be that as it may, the law only protects the *expression* of your idea, not the idea itself. If someone writes about your post in his or her own words, that is perfectly legitimate. In fact, you should welcome it. Consider it free publicity.
2. **Publish an official copyright notice.** This is not required in order to protect your work, nor does it grant you any additional rights. However, it reminds the world that this is your intellectual property. You own it. Using a copyright notice (e.g., "© 2012, Michael Hyatt") can thus serve as a deterrent. I put mine in my blog's footer, so it appears at the bottom of every page.
3. **Create an explicit permissions policy.** Create a separate page spelling out exactly what people may do with your content. I have divided my Permissions Policy[1] into two sections: what others can do without my permission and what they can do with my permission. (See also chapter 55, "Develop a Comments Policy.") Be explicit. This will keep people from contacting you about every use of your content, but it will also give you a published standard to refer to when someone violates it.
4. **Give the benefit of the doubt.** Not everyone who reposts your content does so maliciously. In my experience, most people simply don't know the law. They are not intentionally infringing on your rights. Usually, they are fans who are excited about your work and want to share it with their readers. They are just uninformed about copyright law and need an education.
5. **Request that your post be removed.** You can do this either via e-mail (preferred) or in a comment. Still, be gracious and assume the unauthorized user's motives are good. Don't throttle his enthusiasm. You want him to promote your work; you just don't want him to violate your rights. I start by thanking him for posting it but graciously explain that this is actually illegal. I then point him to my permissions policy and suggest that he post an excerpt instead. In every case, people have apologized to me and complied with my request. (Your mileage may vary.)

6. **Demand that the unauthorized user take down your content.** I have never had to go this far in the online world with my own content. If the offender doesn't respond well to the last step, however, you will need to escalate your response from a request to a demand. You do this by sending a "demand letter" (or e-mail), insisting that the content be taken down. Even here, I would still be gracious (at least the first time), assuming he or she simply doesn't understand the gravity of the situation.

7. **Notify the infringer's hosting service.** If you still can't get the offender to cooperate, you need to do a little research. Find his "WhoIs Record," using a tool like DomainTools.[2] This will show you his domain registration information, including who hosts the site. Then send an e-mail to the hosting service. Usually it is an address like abuse@[the name of the hosting service]. Tell the host you are requesting a "take-down" of the website and explain why. Legitimate services will investigate and, if they agree, send their own demand to the offender. If he doesn't comply, they will take down the site.

8. **Hire an attorney to take action.** If the service provider is shady, incompetent, or offshore, you may need to hire an attorney to represent you. You have to weigh the cost of litigation against the damage you believe is being done. It can get expensive fast, and there is no guarantee of success. Real pirates are incredibly evasive and can disappear and reappear online faster than you can work through the legal process.

The last thing I leave you with on this topic is this: don't let the tail wag the dog. In other words, don't deprive your legitimate audience—the vast majority of your readers—from your content just because you have an occasional person who violates your copyright. It's just not worth it. As I said at the beginning, your biggest problem as a writer is obscurity. The more people reproduce your content, the more people will be exposed to it. Ultimately this will benefit you.

TWENTY-EIGHT

Avoid Common Blogging Mistakes

Assuming you want to increase your blog traffic, there are certain mistakes you must avoid to be successful. If you commit these errors, your traffic will never gain momentum. Worse, it may plateau or begin to decrease.

How do I know? After writing more than twelve hundred posts and receiving almost one hundred thousand comments, I have made most of the mistakes you can make—numerous times. As a result, certain patterns emerged.

These are the top ten traffic killers:

1. **You don't post often enough**. Hobby bloggers may go weeks between posts. But frequency is what separates the men from the boys . . . or the women from the girls. As I've already stressed, you cannot build solid traffic without frequent posts. I have seen time and time again (via Google Analytics) that there is a direct correlation between frequency and traffic. The more I post—within reason—the greater my traffic.[1]

2. **You post too often.** Yes, this is possible too. People don't need to hear from anyone more than once a day—unless it is a group blog or a news site. You would do better to focus on writing one really great post a day rather than several mediocre ones. The trick is to find your frequency sweet spot. For me, it is four to five posts a week.

3. **Your post is too long**. Seth Godin is the master of the short, pithy post. His are usually in the two- to four-hundred-word range. I shoot for

less than five hundred words. But I often post up to six or seven hundred words. Sometimes more. You can get away with this if your posts are scannable—that is, you make use of subheads, lists, and other devices that keep people moving through your content. If a post starts getting too long, consider breaking it up into several posts.

4. **You don't invite engagement.** When I talk about engagement, I am referring to a combination of page views, reader comments, and social media mentions. Postrank.com[2] is one tool for measuring this kind of engagement. The posts that generate the most engagement for me are those that are controversial, transparent (especially about failure), and/or open-ended. This is why I try to end every post with a question.

5. **You don't participate in the conversation.** When bloggers don't participate in the conversation by commenting on their own posts and responding to their readers, it is like hosting a party at your home, making a brief appearance, and then disappearing. In any other context, this behavior would be perceived as rude or odd. The same is true in blogging. People want to have a conversation—with *you*.

6. **You don't make your content accessible.** Since I am in the publishing business (now as a consultant rather than a CEO), I often get asked if I think people are reading less. The simple answer is no. In fact, I think they are reading more than ever. But they are reading differently. Readers have shorter attention spans. They are scanning content, looking for items that interest them.

7. **You don't create catchy headlines.** According to Brian Clark, who runs the must-read site CopyBlogger,[3] "on average, eight out of ten people will read headline copy, but only two out of ten will read the rest." This means your headlines are the most important thing you write. Fortunately, Brian has an entire series of posts called "How to Write Magnetic Headlines."[4] I suggest you read every post.

8. **Your first paragraph is weak.** This is critical. Assuming you have written a great headline, people will next read your first paragraph. You must use this paragraph to pull them into the rest of your blog post. Start with a story, a promise, or a startling fact. The idea is to grab their

attention and hang on to it. Many bloggers spend too much time trying to set up the post or provide context. Just get to the point.

9. **Your post is off-brand.** If you are a hobby blogger, you can get away with the occasional post that strays from your primary message or brand. But if you are trying to build a platform, you need to find an editorial focus and stick to it. A tighter focus leads to higher traffic. This is why I have tried to narrow my own focus to four areas: leadership, productivity, social media, and publishing. If I want to write on something else (e.g., fitness), I do so through one of these four lenses.

10. **Your post is about *you*.** Unless you are a megacelebrity, readers don't care about you. Not really. They care about themselves. They want to know what's in it for *them*. Your personal stories can be a doorway to that, but in the end, the best posts are about your readers' needs, fears, problems, or concerns. Always ask, "What's the takeaway for my reader?"

There are other mistakes too; I doubt this list is exhaustive. But if you can avoid these, you will be well on your way to increasing your traffic and growing your home base.

TWENTY-NINE

Create a Better About Page

When I review my blog's statistics, I am always curious to find out which posts were the most popular. To my surprise, my About page[1] is always among the top ten most visited pages.

Prior to engaging in the review process, I hadn't really thought much about my About page. I viewed it as obligatory, but not really as an opportunity. But obviously anything that is getting clicked on that much is an opportunity.

When you think about it, it makes sense. When we visit a new blog, it is one of the first things we explore. We want to know more about the blogger.

So how can you make your About page better? Here are ten suggestions:

1. **Write in the first person.** Blogs are personal; make your About page personal. You should not write in the third person, as though someone else were writing about you. This is a blog, not a book. Ree Drummond does a great job making her About page warm and casual on her blog, *The Pioneer Woman*:

> Howdy. I'm Ree Drummond, also known as The Pioneer Woman. I'm a moderately agoraphobic ranch wife and mother of four. Welcome to my frontier!
>
> I'm a middle child who grew up on the seventh fairway of a golf course in a corporate town.
>
> I was a teen angel. Not.

> After high school, I thought my horizons needed broadening. I attended college in California, then got a job and wore black pumps to work every day. I ate sushi and treated myself to pedicures on a semi-regular basis. I even kissed James Garner in an elevator once. I loved him deeply, despite the fact that our relationship only lasted 47 seconds.
>
> Unexpectedly, during a brief stay in my hometown, I met and fell in love with a rugged cowboy. Now I live in the middle of nowhere on a working cattle ranch. My days are spent wrangling children, chipping dried manure from boots, washing jeans, and making gravy. I have no idea how I got here . . . but you know what? I love it. Don't tell anyone!
>
> I hope you enjoy my website, ThePioneerWoman.com. Here, I write daily about my long transition from spoiled city girl to domestic country wife.[2]

2. **Write in a conversational style.** People should get a sense of your "voice." If my statistics are representative, this page will be one of the first they visit. They will assume that the style of this page is how you typically write.

3. **Start with the reader's priorities.** Most About pages I have reviewed are written upside down. By this, I mean that the blogger starts with his or her bio, moves on to personal interests, and then (sometimes) gets to what may interest the reader. I suggest you reverse this. Start with the reader's interests.

4. **Tell them about yourself.** This is the first thing I want to know as a reader. But you should resist the temptation to provide your entire bio—at least at the beginning. One or two sentences are sufficient.

5. **Tell them about your blog.** What is your blog about? Try to narrow it down to a theme. For example, my theme is *intentional leadership.* Next explain what kinds of things you write about. I think it is best to limit yourself to a handful of categories. The more focused your content, the more readers you will attract.

   Kate McCulley's About page on *Adventurous Kate's Solo Female*

Travel Blog gives a few fun facts about Kate (she has been shipwrecked and once made a pass at Jon Stewart; she quit her job to travel the world), and then dives right into her theme:

> I am a solo traveler at heart, and one of my goals is to show women that solo travel can be safe, easy, cheap and a lot of fun.
>
> Meanwhile, I'm committed to showing you what the lifestyle of a long-term traveler and online entrepreneur is like. Like anyone else in the world, I have good times and bad times, but I promise to show you reality—with honesty and humor.[3]

6. **Set their expectations**. Tell them how often you post. Don't tell them how often you wish you posted. Instead, tell them how often you actually post. Use an average.
7. **Invite them to subscribe**. In my opinion, this is the most important call to action. You don't want to depend on your readers remembering to return to your blog. Instead, you want them to subscribe so they receive your content every time you post something new.
8. **Point them to your top posts**. This is an opportunity to invite them to "sample the brew." Draw them further into your content. Give them a taste of your best writing. Google Analytics or even your blog's stats package can provide you with a list of your most popular posts of all time. You should also point them to your blog's archive for more content. Adventurous Kate's featured posts include:

   - 11 Best Photos of 2011
   - My Adventurous Travels—From A to Z
   - A Day at the Birmingham Christmas Market
   - A Year in the Life of a Full-Time Traveler
   - How to Tie a Bedouin Scarf[4]

9. **Provide a full biography.** Some of your readers will be more interested in your full bio. This is the place to provide it. You should share your

education, your work history, any books you have written, current interests or hobbies, your family, and so forth. The more you can be a real person, the more people will connect with you.

10. **Tell them how to contact you**. Why hide this? Make it easy. Though it sometimes creates additional work for me, I enjoy hearing from my readers and even answering questions as time permits. (Make it clear what not to contact you about too.) You will also want visitors to follow you on Twitter and Facebook, so provide links to those pages.

Finally, you might want to create a separate About page for your Twitter profile so you can make your page more specific to Twitter followers. This is the page you then link to in your Twitter profile.

While this list provides a top ten, there are a couple of additional items you might want to include. These are, in my opinion, optional:

11. **Include a photo or video**. Since I currently have several on my sidebar already (they rotate with every screen refresh), I don't have a separate one on my About page. If you don't have one there, please do include one on your About page. People want to see what you look like! And, please, if you're forty, don't use your high school graduation picture or a Photoshopped photo. Be authentic. Be real.

    You might also consider adding a short video welcome. This could add even more personality and warmth.

12. **Add a colophon**. Publishers used to add these at the end of books to describe details about the fonts and paper used. You can use it to describe the technologies you are using in your blog (e.g., blogging system, themes, hosting service, and so on), along with design notes about type fonts, photography, and anything else you deem noteworthy. You'd be surprised at how many e-mails I get about these items every week.

13. **Consider a disclaimer**. This is especially important if you work for someone else. You don't want your readers to confuse your blog posts with your company or organization's official position.

Finally, you *must* keep your About page current. I update mine about every three months or so. It's your most important page, so whatever you do, get it right.

Below you'll find my About page,[5] where you'll see many of the elements I discussed in this chapter. The underlined text are hyperlinks on the actual page.

About

I am the chairman of Thomas Nelson Publishers, the largest Christian publishing company in the world and the seventh largest trade book publishing company in the U.S.

This is my personal blog. It is focused on "intentional leadership." My philosophy is if you are going to lead well, you must be thoughtful and purposeful about it.

I write on leadership, productivity, publishing, social media, and, on occasion, stuff that doesn't fit neatly into one of these categories. I also occasionally write about the resources I am discovering.

My goal is to create insightful, relevant content that you can put to work in your personal and professional life. If you are in a position of leadership—or aspire to be—then this blog is for you.

I typically post three to four times a week. To make sure you don't miss my newest posts, you can subscribe via RSS or e-mail. I also accept a limited amount of advertising.

My Top Posts

If you are new to my site, you might want to start with my most popular posts. Here are my top three in each category:

Leadership

- Creating a Life Plan
- The Importance of a Leader's Heart
- Five Characteristics of Weak Leaders

Productivity

- Yes, You Can Stay on Top of E-mail
- How to Shave 10 Hours Off Your Work Week
- Slay Your Dragons Before Breakfast

Publishing

- Advice to First-Time Authors
- Literary Agents Who Represent Christian Authors
- Writing a Winning Book Proposal

Social Media

- Do You Make These 10 Mistakes When You Blog?
- The Beginners Guide to Twitter
- 12 Reasons to Start Twittering

Miscellany

- My Take on the Vibram FiveFingers Running Shoes
- 20 Questions to Ask Other Leaders
- Whatever Happened to Modesty?

You can also check my blog's archive for a list of every post I have written or use the search function below my picture in the sidebar to find other posts that might be of interest.

My Biography

I have worked in the book publishing industry my entire career. I began at Word Publishing while a student at Baylor University. I worked at Word for a total of six years. In addition to serving as vice president of marketing at Thomas Nelson in the mid-80s, I also started my own publishing company, Wolgemuth & Hyatt, with my partner Robert Wolgemuth in 1986. Word eventually acquired our company in 1992.

I was a successful literary agent from 1992 until early 1998. However, I really missed the world of corporate publishing. As a result,

I rejoined Thomas Nelson in 1998. I have worked in a variety of roles in both divisional and corporate management. I was CEO from August 2005 to April 2011, when I was succeeded by Mark Schoenwald. Additionally I am the former chairman of the Evangelical Christian Publishers Association (2006–2010).

I have also written four books, one of which landed on the *New York Times* best-sellers list, where it stayed for seven months. I am currently working on a new book for Thomas Nelson. It is called Platform: Get Noticed in a Noisy World (May 2012).

I have been married to my wife, Gail (follow her on Twitter @GailHyatt), for thirty-three years. We have five daughters, four grandsons, and three granddaughters. We live outside Nashville, Tennessee.

In my free time, I enjoy writing, reading, running, and golfing. I am a member of St. Ignatius Orthodox Church in Franklin, Tennessee, where I have served as a deacon for twenty-three years.

My Contact Information

You can contact me via e-mail or follow me on Twitter or Facebook.

Please note: I do not personally review book proposals or recommend specific literary agents.

Colophon

My blog is built on WordPress 3.1 (self-hosted). My theme is a customized version of Standard Theme, a simple, easy-to-use WordPress theme. Milk Engine did the initial customization. StormyFrog did some additional work. I highly recommend both companies.

In terms of design, the body text font is Georgia. The titles and subhead fonts are Trebuchet MS. Captions and a few other random text elements are Arial. Keely Scott took most of my personal photos. Laurel Pankratz also took some. I get most of the photos for my individual blog posts from iStockPhoto. (You can get a 20 percent discount on stock photos by using the previous link.)

My site is hosted by Linode Cloud. My advertising is handled by Mindy Spradlin at BeaconAds.

Disclaimer

This is my personal blog. The opinions I express here do not necessarily represent those of my employer, Thomas Nelson. The information I provide is on an as-is basis. I make no representations as to accuracy, completeness, currentness, suitability, or validity of any information on this blog and will not be liable for any errors, omissions, or delays in this information or any losses, injuries, or damages arising from its use.

THIRTY

Develop Your Landing Pages

A website landing page highlights one specific product offering, so called because it is the page you want people to land on when you direct them to it from e-mail newsletters, social media, affiliate links, and any other marketing materials.

The goal of the landing page is to convert interest into action. In a sense, it is a salesperson who works for you nonstop—twenty-four hours a day, seven days a week.

For example:

- The Speaking page on my blog is designed to convince meeting planners to book me to speak at their events.[1]
- The "Creating Your Personal Life Plan" page on my blog is designed to convert casual readers into loyal subscribers.[2]
- The "Writing a Winning Book Proposal" page on my blog is designed to sell aspiring authors one or both of my book proposal e-books.[3]

The problem is sometimes landing pages are confusing. Visitors don't know what action to take once they get there. As a result, they don't produce the intended outcome.

If you are launching a new product, service, or cause, you need a landing page. It may be your home page. It may be a separate page altogether (as in my personal examples). But it needs to be a destination.

I have learned the hard way how to create pages that get results. I created a landing page in 2002 that generated over one hundred thousand dollars in the first year. (I can't share a link, because the page is no longer active.) I created a landing page in 2004 that completely failed, generating less than five thousand dollars after a twelve-thousand-dollar investment. (Obviously I took this link down.) I thought that one was a surefire winner.

More recently, I created a landing page for my two e-books, *Writing a Winning Non-Fiction Book Proposal* and *Writing a Winning Fiction Book Proposal*.[4] I sell each e-book separately and together as a bundle.

In the twelve months ending August 31, 2011, I sold 1,097 copies of these e-books for total revenue of $23,730.64. Since the e-books went on sale in October 2009 (two-plus years ago), I have sold a total of 2,239 units for total revenue of $44,681.45. My only costs have been copyediting, typesetting, cover design, and the ongoing payment processing fees.

This is completely passive income. I set up the page, connected it with e-junkie and PayPal, and have done nothing else. The sales, download links, and credit card processing are all handled automatically. The money is automatically deposited to my PayPal account.

Interestingly, these e-books used to generate the same amount every month—about two thousand dollars. Then I decided to analyze the landing page to see if I could improve the conversion. I thought, *If this can generate two thousand dollars a month from a fairly lame landing page, what could it do if I optimized it?* As a result, I completely retooled the page.

The improvement in results was dramatic. I went from generating an average of 3.8 sales a day to 10.6—a 279 percent increase. This is after throwing out the launch-day result of forty-three sales, which I felt was an anomaly. This landing page is now producing annual sales in excess of eighty thousand dollars—not too shabby for a couple of self-published e-books.

Based on my experiences—both positive and negative—I have identified seven characteristics of landing pages that get results:

1. **Headline**. You need a strong, compelling headline. Nothing else on your page is more important than this. If visitors aren't drawn in by the

headline, they won't see everything else. I highly recommend David Garfinkel's book *Advertising Headlines That Make You Rich: Create Winning Ads, Web Pages, Sales Letters and More.*[5] Priceless.

2. **Sales Copy.** You need to write compelling sales copy that starts with your customer's problems and concerns, explains why your product is the solution, and makes a compelling offer. Again, I strongly recommend David Garfinkel. You can't do better than his course *Fast, Effective Copy.*[6] I refer to it weekly. It is expensive but worth every penny. It paid for itself with my very first ad.
3. **Product Photos.** I use BoxShot 3D.[7] It gives you the tools to make your product the hero. For an example, check out the product photos on my *Writing a Winning Book Proposal* product page.

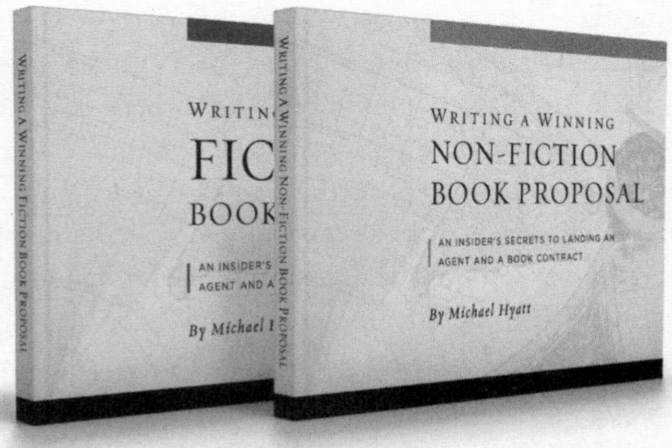

4. **Testimonials.** Nothing convinces people to buy like testimonials. Refer to chapter 14 ("Secure Raving Endorsements") to understand their importance and how to get them. Try to get both celebrity endorsements and user or reader endorsements.
5. **Guarantee.** People may be nervous about buying a product online. They do not know you. There are a thousand and one reasons why they can't pull the trigger. Make it easy. Take the risk out of the transaction. Promise to refund their money promptly if they are not

satisfied. I have only had five refund requests after thousands of sales. If your product is good, it is not a risk.

6. **An Offer.** This is where the rubber meets the road, so to speak. You have to establish a price and make an offer. Don't sell yourself short. I price-tested my e-books at $9.99, $19.99, and $29.99. I actually sold more at $19.99 than $9.99. I think this is partly due to the fact people impute value based on price. If you charge more (within reason), they assume the product is worth more.
7. **Call to Action.** You must ask for the sale. This is known as a call to action. It must be clear, unequivocal, and positioned in a prominent place. I suggest the upper-right-hand corner of the page. Ask yourself, *What is the single action I want visitors to this page to take as a result of reading my copy?* I indicate my call to action with a big red button.

If you are launching a new product, service, or cause, you need a landing page that delivers results. This is essential if you are going to convert readers to customers and, from there, to tribe members.

THIRTY-ONE

Build a Speaking Page

When public speaking became my primary focus, it was time for me to revamp my Speaking page.[1] I highly recommend that you consider public speaking as part of building your platform. It is a great way to raise your visibility, promote your products, and develop credibility with your audience.

Before I began the actual retooling process, I studied the Speaking pages of numerous professional speakers. I noted what I liked—and what I didn't.

Most importantly, I tried to evaluate these pages from the perspective of event sponsors. They are my primary audience. Having been involved in planning hundreds of events through the years, I had a good idea of what is important to them as they are sourcing potential speakers.

Here are the nine action items to create an effective public speaker's landing page. (You might want to open my Speaking page[2] and refer to it as you read about the components below.)

1. **Decide on a call to action.** In other words, what do you want the reader to do after reviewing your page? I used to invite readers to book me (as in "call my booking agents and schedule me for your event"). But now I think that is too much to ask at first.

   Instead, following the lead of some other speakers, I now invite them to check my availability. It's a safer, humbler first step. When they click on the button, they go to a separate page with a brief form. The button looks like this:

Check My Availability

I also made the call-to-action button red to stand out from everything else on my blog and placed it in the upper-right-hand corner of the page, where I knew it wouldn't be missed. (This is arguably the most important real estate on your page.) I also put a few other iterations of this button in the actual page text.

2. **Create a one-minute welcome video**. Don't make this complicated. My wife, Gail, and I shot mine in my study at home. Your goal is to create empathy with the viewer (i.e., the event sponsor) and provide a personalized preview of what is on the page—that is, your intro copy.

   In case you are interested, I used a Canon 60D camera on a tripod and an Audio-Technica ATR 3350 lavaliere microphone with a mono-to-stereo adapter from Radio Shack. I did not use any special lighting.

An iPad 2 served as my teleprompter, and I used the Proprompter HDi Pro2 from Bodelin Technologies.

I edited the video in iMovie and then uploaded it to Vimeo, which I like much better than YouTube. It has many more options, including the ability to use a minimalist video player and custom thumbnail image.

3. **Provide an overview of the page.** Arrange the sections in the order that make the most sense to you. For my page, I also solicited the advice of my booking agents, who made some excellent suggestions.

Regardless, you want event sponsors to be able to navigate the page in whatever order makes sense to them. Some may want to go first to the most requested topics. Others may want to see the video clips first.

What You Can Expect
A Little Bit About Me
My Video Clips
My Most Requested Topics
What Others Are Saying
My Upcoming Engagements
My Previous Engagements
The Next Step

Create a list of the subheads and then hyperlink them to the actual sections. That way they can navigate the page in whatever order they choose and always come back to this index by clicking on the "Return to Top" link at the bottom of each section.

Explain what a potential buyer can expect. When someone buys a product, he is not just purchasing an artifact. He is buying an experience. The same is true in booking a speaker. Event sponsors are purchasing not only a speech but the entire experience around the speech.

This includes:

- The ways in which your booking agents interact with the sponsor, including the promptness of their replies.
- The first interaction with you via a preconference call.
- Your promotion of the event (assuming the sponsor wants that) via your blog and social media networks.
- A custom resource page for all the event attendees. It includes a copy of the slide deck you used in the presentation (embedded with SlideShare.net[3]), along with links to books, blog posts, and other resources you believe will be helpful.

- A quick follow-up with the sponsor after the event to make sure you hit the target.

4. **Write a specialized biography.** On my old Speaking page, I simply cut and pasted the copy from the About section of my blog. However, as I passed this through the filter of what's-important-to-an-event-planner, I realized it needed to be totally rewritten.

Start with your speaking experience. Add some of your media experience, including any of the more noteworthy TV and radio shows you have been on. In my case, the interesting fact is the sheer volume. I have been on more than twelve hundred shows.

Next present your credentials, including your career history and the scope of your social media platform. End with a brief personal paragraph about your family and personal interests. This puts a human face on the bio.

5. **Assemble a collection of video clips.** This may be the most important section. Event sponsors want to know how you come across in front of a live audience.

You should ask every sponsor to record your presentation on video. Many won't be able to, but you'd be surprised how many will if you just ask. You are looking for one- to two-minute moments that represent you in a live context.

I also had SimplyVideo[4] take all my recordings and create a quick, two-and-a-half-minute video demo. This is something that sponsors can use with their committees or other decision makers. I was very pleased with the SimplyVideo process and ultimate product.

A Short Demo Video

This is a quick demo video:

In a Corporate Environment

Here are some examples of me speaking in a corporate context.

You can find even more video clips by clicking here.

6. **Compile a list of your most requested topics.** This may take quite a bit of work. I had to go back through the last three years of speaking and identify the topics that were the most popular and I felt were congruent with my brand.

   When you have your list, write a brief description of each topic, then find a photo you feel is iconic for each talk. I found mine through iStockPhoto.com.[5] I think the visual element is critical. I downloaded the photos and created a slideshow in iWork Keynote. I then exported each slide to create the thumbnails for this section.

MY MOST REQUESTED TOPICS

I speak on topics related to leadership, life balance, productivity, and social media. I will customize my presentation to meet your organization's specific needs. My goal is to facilitate the outcome *you* want to create.

My most requested topics include the following ones. Keep in mind that I can present these as a keynote or a workshop. Also, I have a half-day, and in some cases, full-day seminar version.

Platform: In today's hyper-noisy world, it is hard to get anyone's attention. You need a platform to be seen and heard. Thankfully, it's never been easier. In this presentation, I discuss how to use social media to build your brand, decrease your marketing costs, and increase your impact.

Creating Your Personal Life Plan: Few people have a plan for their life. Most are passive spectators, watching their life unfold, one day at a time. In this presentation, I explain how to go from reactive to *proactive* and develop a plan for accomplishing those priorities that matter most.

Shift: Everything is changing: the economy, demographics, social media—and what our teams expect from us as leaders. In this presentation, I outline seven changes leaders must make to be effective in a post-modern world. We can't go back to the way things were. This is the New Normal.

7. **Collect endorsements from previous sponsors.** These are important as well. Endorsements provide third-party validation. Others are able to say things about you that you could never say about yourself.

As a matter of procedure, always ask sponsors to provide an endorsement immediately after you speak. This is when your speech is the most fresh in their minds. It is also the point at which they are the most excited and likely to write a testimonial.

I use the endorsements in two ways. I provide the full endorsement in the right-hand sidebar. Then I boil down the endorsement to the crème de la crème and include them in a WordPress "slider" in the main body copy. I used NivoSlider[6] for this. It looks like this:

"He held an arena of 8,000 college students spellbound."

—JOHNNIE MOORE
Vice President and Campus Pastor
Liberty University

• • • • ○ • • • • • •

8. Insert a calendar of upcoming events. As a speaker, the busier your calendar is the better. It demonstrates you are in demand. This helps validate the claims you are making elsewhere.

I used to use a WordPress plugin called GigPress,[7] which I still recommend. It is excellent. However, for this iteration of my Speaking page, I had my Web developer write some custom code. I wanted to be able to announce each engagement via a minipost on my blog and then have that post automatically included on my calendar.

Date		Topic / Event Details		City / More Info
—	**09/15/2011** 07:30–8:30 a.m.	**Keynote:** "How to Go Further, Faster"		**Cle Elum, WA**
		Event:	Building Champions Experience 2011	Public Event
		Sponsor:	Building Chapions	Register to attend
		Venue:	Suncadia Resort 3600 Suncadia Trail Cle Elum, WA 98922 United States	Get more information
+	**09/15/2011** 11:15–12:15 p.m.	**Workshop:** "How to Shave 10 Hours Off Your Work Week"		**Cle Elum, WA**
+	**09/15/2011** 09:30–11:00 a.m.	**Keynote:** "Making a Greater Difference Outside the Office"		**Cle Elum, WA**
+	**10/05/2011** 02:15–03:30 p.m.	**Workshop:** "The Importance of the Leader's Heart"		**Duluth, GA**

I also wanted to show the full list of engagements, providing the event planner (or someone just interested in hearing me speak) with the ability to expand the event and see more detail.

9. **Include a picture of you speaking.** Visually, it is important for event sponsors to see you in action. You want a picture of you having fun in front of a big audience. This enables sponsors to visualize you in front of their audience. It is important to have a professional photographer take the picture.

   Think carefully about what you want to portray in the picture, then communicate to the photographer what you are after. Ask him or her to take plenty of audience shots as well.

The goal with each of these tips is to make it as easy as possible for people to decide to book you to speak. My friend Ken Davis, a comedian, goes the extra mile making it easy.[8] In addition to many of the things we've already covered in this chapter, he includes some extra items as a part of his Booking page that make promoting his events almost turnkey for anyone who books him.

Using the tools on Ken's site, event sponsors can send out custom e-mail invitations to their events. They can download photos, customizable press releases, printable posters, and audio and video clips to use in their promotions. And Ken even makes available free website banners, WordPress widgets, and targeted pop-in banners for sponsors to use on their websites. And finally, he offers sponsors a short URL they can use to let people know about the event. Like Ken, you may have some creative ideas that will make it easy for event sponsors to click on that call-to-action button.

If you are including public speaking in your platform-building plans, I suggest that you incorporate most—or all—of these tips in your Speaking page. Consider adding your own creative touch too.

THIRTY-TWO

Forget About Metrics (for Now)

A few years ago, my blog readership plateaued for a couple of months. (We'll cover blog metrics in chapter 41). The number of my monthly visitors had been relatively flat. For someone whose primary strength is "achiever," this was a bitter pill to swallow. I immediately thought, *What am I doing wrong?*

If you're like me, you like starting things. You like growing things. You do not like maintaining things. It's just how many of us are wired. If the numbers aren't moving in a positive direction, we get frustrated and can lose interest.

Frankly, this has forced me to reevaluate why I am blogging. We each have our own reasons. One young blogger said this: "If we give some good stuff to other people, we might get some good stuff back, like nice comments, or someone answering a question we've asked, or telling us something really good we didn't know about."[1] That makes some sense to me.

In the past, I have said I blog for five reasons: 1) to raise my organization's visibility; 2) to articulate my organization's vision; 3) to network with people who can help me; 4) to be alert to what my constituents are saying; and 5) to mentor the next generation of leaders.

But the more I have thought about it, I've concluded these are really the benefits of blogging, not the reasons. The reality is, I blog in order to clarify my thinking and archive my best ideas. In short, I blog for me. (But you are welcome to read along!)

It shouldn't make any difference whether you have ten readers or one hundred thousand. Dawson Trotman, the founder of the Navigators, had it right decades ago when he said, "Thoughts disentangle themselves when they pass through the lips and fingertips."[2] If you are writing, you are achieving greater clarity about your life, your work, and what matters most. That's enough. And more than most people have.

===

Your home base is the heart of your platform, and getting it right the first time will set you up for success. In this section we've walked through some valuable information I learned mostly the hard way. I hope it will save you some pain and suffering. Now let's turn to the next step—expanding your reach.

PART FOUR

EXPAND YOUR REACH

THIRTY-THREE

Kiss Marketing Good-Bye

When you saw the title to this chapter, you may have wondered why I start a section about expanding your reach with a headline about getting rid of marketing. After all, you want to learn how to build a platform and make it a powerful one, with lots of followers.

It takes marketing to do that, right? And isn't marketing what you hire other people to do? It's PR people making pitch calls or ad agencies spending big bucks creating snazzy magazine ads. Or for those of us who don't have the money to do that, it might be making our own fliers and taking out small ads in the local paper. Perhaps buying an occasional radio ad.

Whatever it looks like, most creatives I know hate marketing. They want to build things, innovate new products, write, speak, or entertain. But they hate the thought of promoting themselves or selling their products and services.

If this describes you, I have good news. Marketing is dead.

Okay, maybe I am overstating my case.

Marketing may not be dead, but, in the world of social media, it has morphed. Dramatically.

Tribe-building is the new marketing.

Marketing is no longer about shouting in a crowded marketplace; it is about participating in a dialogue with fellow travelers. Marketing is no longer about generating transactions; it is about building relationships. Marketing is no longer about exploiting a market for your own benefit; it is about serving those who share your passion—for your mutual benefit.

In his groundbreaking book *Tribes: We Need You to Lead Us*,[1] Seth Godin defines a tribe as "a group of people connected to one another, connected to a leader, and connected to an idea."

I read this book right after it came out in 2008, and it is just as relevant today as it was then. It is must reading if you are serious about building an enduring career as a creative.

Godin says that a tribe only has two requirements: a shared interest and a way to communicate.

It is easy to think of examples:

- **Apple Users**. Just visit a local Apple retail store. People aren't just there to buy products. They come to share their passion and interact with other enthusiasts. While other retailers struggle, Apple can barely keep up with the demand.
- **Dave Ramsey Fans**. Ramsey has built an immense tribe of people who are passionate about getting out of debt and taking control of their money. It borders on religious fervor. No wonder. His philosophy has given hope to millions.
- **Don Miller Readers**. His first book, *Blue Like Jazz*,[2] was on the *New York Times* best-sellers list for months. He tried to make a movie based on the book but couldn't raise the money. But his tribe wouldn't let it die. They raised the money themselves.
- **Evernote Users**. Who would ever think that a simple software database would engender such a large and burgeoning tribe? But with over twelve million registered users, Evernote has attracted a diverse and passionate group of users.

I am a proud member of all four tribes.

But here's the key for creatives: building a tribe is your ticket to enduring success. This is what platform is all about. It is a way for you to connect to your tribe.

How do you build a tribe? Let me suggest four ways:

1. **Discover your passion.** Marketing is the act of sharing what you are passionate about. Nothing more. Nothing less.

   For example, Gary Vaynerchuk started Wine Library TV.[3] Though he no longer posts there, he built a huge tribe that didn't exist when he began in 2006. It started when he discovered his passion for wine.

   Millions of people tuned into Gary's short video program daily to discover new wines and better understand the wines they love. He has moved on to bigger and better things, but his initial effort is a testimony to what can be done when someone discovers his passion.

2. **Volunteer to lead.** This is everything. Without a leader, you don't have a tribe. You only have a crowd.

   Marketing is really about leading people who already want to follow. They just need a leader to take them where they already want to go.

3. **Be generous.** The old marketing was about taking from people. As it turns out, "It is more blessed to give than to receive"[4] is a brilliant marketing strategy. When you lead by serving and by giving, people follow.

4. **Provide a way to communicate.** People need a way to communicate. They need a way to share their stories.

   In *Tribes*, Seth outlines four kinds of tribal leadership. If you are going to be serious about building tribes, you have to provide for all four kinds of communication.

   - Tribe leader to tribe member
   - Tribe member to tribe leader
   - Tribe member to tribe member
   - Tribe member to outsiders

The real issue is no longer whether or not your publishing company or record label—or any other third party—will market your product and give you the visibility you need to succeed. It is really about whether or not you are willing to step up and provide leadership to a tribe of fellow travelers who share your passion.

THIRTY-FOUR

Understand What's *Not* Important

Some time ago, in preparation for a meeting with one of my biggest clients, I visited his website. He wanted to extend the reach of his platform, and I was consulting with him. I was reminded again how many businesspeople think that by just hanging a website in cyberspace they are somehow building their brand. As it turns out, not so much.

The site looked great. Nice graphics. Cool use of Flash. Lots of razzle-dazzle. So I decided to run his site through HubSpot's Marketing Grader.[1] This simple, free tool is like a CAT scan for websites. It is very revealing—and my client's site scored poorly.

Based on my newfound data, I decided to do a little research. I next ran my top twelve clients' websites through the same exercise. As you look at the results in the chart below, keep in mind:

- **Overall Web Grade** is the WebsiteGrader.com grade. It is based on a complex set of criteria, including the items below.
- **Google Page Rank** shows Google's relative rank on a one to ten scale. The higher the number, the better.
- **Alexa Traffic Rank** shows your absolute traffic ranking against all other websites in the world. It's similar to the Nielsen ratings. The lower the number, the better. For example, the first client's rank below—18,977—means its site is in the top twenty thousand sites in the world. Since there are tens of millions, this is impressive.

- **Technorati Page Rank** shows absolute traffic ranking against all other blog sites in the world. If the blog is not registered with Technorati, then it is not ranked. The lower the number, the better.

Here are the results:

Client	Overall Web Grade	Google Page Rank	Alexa Traffic Rank	Technorati Page Rank
Client 1	99.9	6	18,977	1,218
Client 2	99.3	6	110,308	726,714
Client 3	93.0	5	52,288	N/A
Client 4	92.0	5	393,576	20,212
Client 5	91.0	5	427,192	N/A
Client 6	89.0	4	613,492	N/A
Client 7	86.0	4	674,324	213,437
Client 8	86.0	4	257,410	N/A
Client 9	82.0	4	402,066	N/A
Client 10	81.0	5	545,916	N/A
Client 11	79.0	4	548,447	N/A
Client 12	35.0	3	3,738,452	N/A

Here are my conclusions:

1. **Having a really slick, graphically clever website does not necessarily correlate with more traffic.** In fact, the ones that made use of the latest Flash and embedded video technologies scored at the low end of the traffic scale.
2. **Having a large media platform does not necessarily correlate with more traffic.** Yes, the president of Client 1 has a huge media platform on

both TV and radio. However, one of the clients with the biggest media platforms was dead last.

3. **Having a large organization behind you does not necessarily correlate with more traffic.** Some clients with large organizations were near the top; some were near the bottom.
4. **Having a young and hip image does not necessarily correlate with more traffic.** In fact, there seems to be an inverse correlation. Maybe the older people work harder at it. Perhaps the younger ones think being cool is enough. Regardless, most of the ones I assumed would be web-savvy are not—at least in terms of generating meaningful traffic.

I'd suggest you run your own site or blog through Marketing Grader. This will give you a good snapshot of where you are now.

For the sake of transparency, I'll share my own numbers with you. Here are my Marketing Grader results as of this writing:

	Overall Web Grade	**Google Page Rank**	**Alexa Traffic Rank**	**Techorati Page Rank**
MichaelHyatt.com	99.3	5	19,200	618

Note: these will fluctuate slightly because many of the rankings are relative. If someone's site becomes more popular and outranks you, your site will move down. The opposite is also true.

The good news is, it is not that difficult to build a powerful online presence. Nor does it cost much. It's definitely worth the time you'll invest.

THIRTY-FIVE

Generate More Blog Traffic

In a recent thirty-day period, I watched my blog traffic jump by 81.3 percent. In fact, I have seen steady growth since I converted from TypePad to self-hosted WordPress[1] a few years ago (up 338.6 percent). But that thirty days represented the largest single jump in my traffic ever, according to my Google Analytics report.[2]

I believe there are some clear reasons why this happened.

For one thing, this traffic increase wasn't the result of a single post that caught fire. Nor was it the result of a large site linking to me. Rather, it was the result of several specific changes I made to my blog. Even here, I don't think it was a single change, but rather all of them working together that accounted for the impact on traffic. The good news is these are things *you* can replicate.

First, the facts—directly from Google Analytics. (By the way, if you don't have this installed on your blog, do that first. It's easy, free, and essential if you are serious about growing your traffic.)

- Absolute unique visitors went from 71,885 to 130,320 in one month (an 81.3 percent increase).
- Page views went from 173,794 to 284,192 (a 63.5 percent increase).

What did I do to make this happen?

As we've discussed in previous chapters, I had already decided to install Standard Theme (a WordPress theme for serious bloggers).[3] This had an immediate, positive impact on my traffic. This was due primarily to faster page-load times and better Search Engine Optimization (SEO). Other bloggers I know have had similar results from this premium theme.

Then I asked myself, *What actions can I take to significantly grow my blog traffic*? I came up with a list of four:

1. **Increase blogging frequency.** I have always known there is a correlation between frequency and growth in traffic, but I proved it to myself empirically. For most of last year, I posted three times a week. I decided I would post five times a week, Monday through Friday.
2. **Write shorter posts, shorter paragraphs, and shorter sentences.** I owe this insight to a post at CopyBlogger called "Shorter Is Better."[4] I determined to keep my posts between five and six hundred words. Each paragraph would include no more than three to four sentences. And I would avoid compound sentences wherever possible.
3. **Improve my SEO metadata.** I started using Scribe.[5] This WordPress plug-in analyzes your posts and gives you a score, based on how Google will rank it. Best of all, it tells you how to tweak your metadata to improve your score. It's expensive, but I think it's worth every penny.
4. **Become more engaged in comments.** I changed my commenting system from native WordPress to Disqus.[6] This is the system used by most of the larger sites I visit. I believe it is the easiest, most elegant commenting plugin available. It also allows me to reply to comments via e-mail, which makes it super easy to engage with my readers.

The results were encouraging. But there is no silver bullet that will instantly generate more traffic. It takes doing several things right—and doing them over a long period of time.

I have used the following basic techniques to increase my blog traffic every year since I started tracking it in 2008 using Google Analytics. Some years have been better than others, but all have shown an increase:

Year	Pageviews	Increase
2008	574,778	N/A

2009	1,496,241	160.3%
2010	1,972,497	31.8%
2011	5,060,331	156.5%

Based on my experience, I believe you can dramatically increase your blog traffic by following these ten fundamental suggestions. (We've already discussed some of them in other contexts, but they bear repeating.)

- **Write content worth sharing.** Nothing will compensate for weak content. If you are not writing stuff people want to read, smarter marketing will not fix the problem. Begin by creating a killer headline that makes people want to read what you have to say. Read *Advertising Headlines That Make You Rich.*[7] It's my secret sauce.
- **Adhere to a consistent schedule.** You can't expect to increase your traffic if you don't blog regularly. By this, I mean at least once a week. Three times a week is even better. Five is best—but not if the quality of your content suffers. Frequency equals visibility.
- **Get your own domain name.** Make it easy on your readers to pass along your blog name. What do you think is easier, "yourname.wordpress.com" or "yourname.com"? This is the foundation of branding, and it makes your blog *memorable.* If you can get your name or a short phrase, it is worth paying (within reason) to do so.
- **Include your blog address everywhere.** In the beginning, you are adding readers one at a time. You never know when someone with a bigger audience will quote you or link to you. Include your blog address in your e-mail signature, on your business cards, and on your stationary. It should appear virtually everywhere your name appears, particularly in your social media profiles.
- **Make it easy to subscribe to your blog.** You don't want to depend on your readers to remember to come back to your blog. Instead, you want them to subscribe, so they get every new post you write. They should be able to do so by either RSS or e-mail. Use both. Position these two buttons prominently.

- **Optimize your posts for SEO**. You want people to be able to find you when they search one of your keywords or your name. I use two WordPress plugins for this: All-in-One SEO Pack[8] and Scribe.[9] The former assists you in optimizing your metadata (i.e., post title, description, and tags). The latter assists you in optimizing the post itself.
- **Utilize social media**. If you want to build visibility for your blog, you must go where the people are. In days gone by, people gathered in the marketplace at the center of the city. Today, they gather online in places like Twitter, Facebook, LinkedIn, and Google+. Which service is best? *The one you will use regularly*. Use social media to network, build relationships, and announce new blog posts.
- **Engage in the conversation**. Start by making it easy for your readers to comment. People today want to participate. Don't make them register. This only adds friction. Engage in the conversation yourself, reading your comments and replying as appropriate.
- **Comment on other blogs**. As you read other people's blog posts, leave comments. I'm not talking about spamming people with invitations to read your blog. Instead, engage in the conversations that interest you and build credibility. Make sure you register with their commenting system, so there is always a link back to your blog.
- **Write guest posts for other bloggers**. Frankly, this is not something I have done. But most successful bloggers swear by it. Jeff Goins wrote a guest post[10] for me on this very subject. He claims it grew his own blog traffic more in six months than in the previous six years. (If you are interested in guest posting on my site, check out my Guidelines page.[11])

You will also want to use a good, SEO-optimized blog theme. There are hundreds on the market. As I've mentioned, I use Standard Theme for WordPress and love it.

Finally, be patient. Building traffic takes time. Like anything else, the ones who win are the ones who stay at it after everyone else has quit.

THIRTY-SIX

Build Your Subscriber List

The goal of marketing is to attract more customers. Businesses make an enormous investment to get people in the doors the first time. But what happens after that?

If the customer walks out the door, never to return, the investment is wasted. "Blood on the ground," as they say. Instead, marketers want the customer to come back—and, they hope, bring a few friends.

The same is true in the world of blogging. I have never yet met a blogger who didn't want more traffic. *Writers write to be read!* (Anyone who tells you different is lying.)

If that's true for you, then you need to stop focusing on growing your traffic. Instead, you need to concentrate on *growing your subscriber list.*

Why? Because this list represents your hard-core followers—the ones who are most likely to recruit other readers. This means you don't have to do it on your own. It is the difference between addition and multiplication.

Recently, I realized that I had been guilty of this myself. As we discussed in the last chapter, I grew my traffic—which is a necessary first step to expanding your reach—but wasn't paying attention to growing my *list.* I made the RSS button prominent and thought that was enough.

But after reading the advice of several professional bloggers, I realized that I needed to focus on building an e-mail subscription list. From the blogger's perspective, an e-mail list provides bloggers with several advantages over RSS subscriptions:

- **It is more personal.** With e-mail, you know who your subscribers are. It also moves the conversation from the impersonal world of RSS readers to the more personal environment of your reader's in-box.
- **It provides more control.** If Google has a glitch and deletes all your RSS subscribers . . . they are gone. There's no way to get them back. With the e-mail list management program, you can back up your subscribers on a regular basis.
- **It enables two-way communication.** I use my real address when I send out my e-mail newsletter. If you do this, it will enable people to reply and give you feedback. That e-mail will come straight to you and allows you to respond if necessary.
- **It enables you to track your effectiveness.** With RSS, you know how many people subscribe but not much beyond this. With e-mail list software, you have access to numerous reports. For example, you will know how many actually opened the e-mail, clicked on the links, unsubscribed, and so on.
- **It gives you the opportunity to promote products.** With RSS, you have to write a blog post to communicate with your subscribers. With e-mail, you can send out a communiqué any time you want.
- **It provides an easy way to share your content.** If, like me, you have a lot of readers who share your posts on Facebook and Twitter, be grateful. But realize that you still have thousands of readers who don't use social media. With e-mail, they can simply forward it to their friends.

Okay, so how do you actually build your e-mail subscriber list? Let me tell you what I did.

In March 2011, I had 2,771 e-mail subscribers. I didn't think it was very impressive, given the fact that I was getting about 150,000 unique visitors a month at the time. I didn't seem to be converting many readers into subscribers.

However, in the last nine months, I have grown my list to more than 50,000 e-mail subscribers (as of this writing). In the same period of time,

I have doubled my blog's traffic, reaching more than 310,000 unique visitors a month.

Here are the seven strategies I used to grow my e-mail subscriber list:

1. **Generate content worth reading.** I've said it before, but I can't emphasize it enough. No one will subscribe to anything they don't want to read. You have to write quality content—and leave readers wanting more.
2. **Use a dedicated list subscription system.** You can use Google's free FeedBurner service. In fact, I do use that for RSS. But it doesn't provide the same level of control you get with paid services like MailChimp[1] or AWeber.[2] I use MailChimp. It's a little pricey, but I love the control.
3. **Make your sign-up form highly visible.** At the very least, it should be "above the fold" (on the upper half of the page) preferably in the right-hand sidebar. Take a look at how the sign-up form is positioned on the CopyBlogger[3] or ProBlogger[4] sites.
4. **Offer an incentive for subscribing.** This is where creativity comes in. A good example is Hugh MacLeod, who draws cartoons. When his doodles became popular, he started expanding his reach through his blog, *gapingvoid*.[5] If you subscribe, you get to start five mornings a week with "Hugh's Daily Cartoon" absolutely free. Hugh describes it as "a wee chuckle in your inbox, to start your day off on the right foot (so to speak)."[6]

   This "free" concept was huge for me. I wrote an e-book called *Creating Your Personal Life Plan* and offered it free to anyone who would sign up.[7] If you want to consider doing something similar, you could start with a series of posts you have written. Just format it as an e-book.
5. **Design a branded e-mail template.** For my purposes, I hired a developer to design an e-mail template in MailChimp. If you do the same thing, remember it is important that the branding elements match your blog. Built-in social media buttons are a must, so people can share your posts with their friends and followers. You want your subscribers to feel they are getting a high-quality product.

6. **Follow up with your subscribers.** I use MailChimp's auto-responder feature to send out a welcome message after they confirm their subscription. This is where you thank them for subscribing and tell them what to expect. After three weeks, send out another message, again thanking them and inviting them to share your posts with their friends. By this time, hopefully, they have found value in what you write.
7. **Remind your readers to sign up.** My pop-up disappears after the first three times a reader visits. (I think it gets annoying after this.) I recommend you insert a sign-up form at the bottom of each post. This serves as a reminder once they have finished reading the post. It may take some people several posts before they get comfortable subscribing.

Your tactics may vary, depending on where you are as a blogger. Still, the principles are applicable at every level. With a little focused effort—and perhaps a modest investment of time and money—you can dramatically increase the number of people who subscribe to your blog.

THIRTY-SEVEN

Promote Your Older Posts

As a blogger, you'll find that your older, archived posts typically don't get a lot of attention. The reading public tends to focus on what is new and notable, rather than what is tried and true. If you aren't intentional about it, your older posts will sink into your archives, only to be discovered when someone happens to search for one of the keywords used in the post or metadata. (This is one good reason to make sure that each post is optimized for the search engines.)

Not too long ago, I decided to become intentional about promoting my older posts. As a result of the actions I took, they began to account for more and more of my daily traffic. In fact, today they account for about 30 to 40 percent of my total traffic. In effect you can expand your reach by using material you've already sweated over!

Here's what I did—and what you can do—to give your older posts new life:

1. **Identify your most popular posts.** You can use your blogging software's statistics feature or Google Analytics.[1] This is one way of crowdsourcing your best content. Give your readers a vote! And don't be afraid to include some of your personal favorites, even if they aren't your top traffic generators. It's worth experimenting. I created a list of my top one hundred. But even twenty or thirty would be a good start.
2. **Make sure each post is still relevant.** Quickly review each post. Update statistics or references to current events. Try to make the post as timeless as possible. I switched blog designs and found that I had to resize

my photos to fit the new format. I did the bulk of this work one Saturday morning. It was well worth the investment of time.

3. **Move your post date to the bottom of the post.** Sadly, many readers will dismiss something as irrelevant just because you wrote it last year. Because of this, you should move the post date from the top of the post, where it screams for attention, to the bottom, where it is less conspicuous. I have not had a single complaint about this.[2]
4. **Write a Twitter post for each blog post.** Create a new text file, listing each of your top blog posts. Then write a separate Twitter status update corresponding to each post, using an intriguing question or fact as a lead-in. I recommend keeping the Twitter post under 120 characters to make it easier for your followers to retweet. Also, use a URL shortener (like bit.ly) and make it clear it is a repost. Here are some examples from my top blog posts file:

> Where does social media fit into your strategy? Here is a simple, 3-part model I have found helpful. Repost: http://bit.ly/bv7WfP
>
> Why is keeping your word so important, even if you don't have a contract? Here are 3 reasons. Repost: http://bit.ly/aWmiRA
>
> Okay, you're working more hours than you would like. Here are 10 reasons why you aren't done yet. Repost: http://bit.ly/axXXKT
>
> I believe that the essence of leadership is expressed in one word: SHIFT. It has 3 different components. Repost: http://bit.ly/9vJBkW
>
> As a leader, how do you create alignment in your organization? Here are three strategies. Repost: http://bit.ly/d8nLlh

5. **Schedule the tweets using an automated system.** This is an optional step, but one I recommend. You could just cut and paste from your top blog posts file to Twitter, say, once a day. But if you join a service like SocialOomph.com,[3] you can actually schedule posts as far into the future as you want. In fact, you can upload your entire text file, telling SocialOomph to schedule one post a day at a specific time. I run

one a day at 11:00 a.m. With ninety posts, it takes ninety days before a Twitter post will be repeated.

6. **Include your top ten blog posts on your About page.** This page is more important than you think. I recommend using a custom About page as your main link on your Twitter profile page. You shouldn't force new readers to go hunting for posts to read. Instead, as a good host, point them to your most popular posts.
7. **Create a sidebar list of your most popular posts.** Many themes, like WooThemes,[4] have this feature built in. It will either automatically display your most popular posts or allow you to populate it with the ones you want to make more visible. Personally, I like to be able to edit the list and rotate it from time to time.
8. **Respond to those who comment.** I keep mentioning this because engaging with your readers in the comments section of your blog is extremely important. People today don't visit a blog to listen to a monologue. They want to be part of a conversation. Therefore, you should engage in new comments on old posts, as if the post were brand-new—and it is for those readers. It's a good way to set the tone and let them know what to expect in the future.
9. **Don't overdo it.** This is critical. If you are constantly tweeting or Facebooking links to your own posts, people will feel they are getting spammed. I have tried various frequencies and found that one top blog post a day is about right. I have never had any complaints. For a while, I experimented with two a day and received several complaints. So be helpful without being annoying.

The best thing about the Internet is that your content is never unavailable. But that doesn't mean people will find it or that it will command attention. To keep your older blog posts from dying in your archives, you have to be intentional and strategic.

THIRTY-EIGHT

Write Guest Posts

My friend Jeff Goins wrote a terrific guest post on my blog about—what else—guest posting! Guest posting is a great way to expand your reach. Here is Jeff's post in its entirety (with his permission, of course). Do yourself a favor and subscribe to his blog.[1]

Although I've been blogging since 2005, I still feel like a newbie sometimes. For years I've wondered, *Why is nobody reading what I'm writing?* Maybe you've asked the same question.

I'm beginning to discover the answer. It has to do with community.

I've stumbled upon a secret: blogging is communal, and those who participate in the community win.

My blog readership and influence has grown more in the past six months than it has in the past six years. Why? Because I've been guest-posting more in the past six months than I have in the past six years.

Most bloggers spin their wheels trying to increase traffic on their own blogs, while overlooking the essential discipline of writing guest posts for other blogs. Nothing can grow your platform quite like it.

Consider the following bloggers: Leo Babauta (of Zen Habits),[2] Brian Clark (of CopyBlogger),[3] and Chris Brogan (of Chrisbrogan.com).[4] All have used guest-posting as a means of growing the reach of their blogs. And you can too.

Guest posting is great for search engines, introduces you to new communities (and them to you), and allows your ideas to spread more freely.

This is an essential marketing strategy for any blogger, but few know how to do it well.

Here are seven steps to successful guest-posting:

1. **Check the guidelines.** Many established blogs have a list of guidelines that you can follow to make a guest post. Before submitting your post, read the guidelines and follow them.
2. **Study the blog.** Do some research to understand the subject and voice of the blog and to see what topics haven't been covered yet. If you know someone who has guest-posted for the blog, ask him how he did it.
3. **Contact the blogger.** E-mail is probably best. In the message, get right to the point. Either pitch an idea or send the whole article, but don't waste time with unnecessary flattery or self-deprecation. Don't say sorry, and don't be arrogant. Just be yourself.
4. **Write the best post you can.** (This may happen concurrently with number 3). Once you've made contact with the blogger, you can begin writing. Fight the temptation to hold back your "A" content for your own blog. Guest posts are your best marketing collateral, so don't submit something less than your best. Once finished, send the ready-to-publish post to the blogger with a byline and link to your website.
5. **Follow up.** Depending on the guidelines, give the blogger some time (usually a week) before following up. When you do follow up, keep it positive and polite. You can follow up again a week or two later. If you don't hear back in a month, tell the blogger that you'd like to take the article elsewhere.
6. **Engage and promote.** If the blogger posts your article, first thank her. Then treat it as you would one of your own posts, if not better. Tweet it, share it, e-mail it, and so forth. Post an excerpt on your own blog and link to the whole article. Interact in the comments and engage readers who respond. This is a must.
7. **Repeat.** Whether you succeed or not, start the whole process over again. If you get rejected, don't get discouraged. And don't let it be

the last time you try to guest post. Sometimes, the topic is just wrong. Other times, it's the wrong audience. Regardless, you need to guest post more than once for it to be an effective strategy. So don't give up.

One final thought: If the blogger is local (or a traveler), try meeting up with him for coffee. The best blogging relationships are birthed out of relationship.

The most elite bloggers on the Internet have grown their blog readerships through this simple, but effective strategy of guest posting. And you can grow your blog by doing the same.

═

This is good advice. I currently run one guest post on my blog each week. The bloggers who have participated in this often report their biggest traffic day ever. But it is also a huge help to me: it is one less post I have to write and it gives my audience some variety. The bottom line: it's a win for both of us—and the online community.

THIRTY-NINE

Give Stuff Away

In the 2000s, we witnessed the "free revolution." Marketers gave away everything from books and software to vacations and even cars. This has shaped consumer behavior to the point that people often expect free and resent having to pay.

Free is certainly not a viable long-term business model. Nonetheless, it can be a brilliant marketing strategy, as we've discussed. Many individuals and companies are using this strategy very effectively to:

- **Build mailing lists.** As I mentioned in a previous chapter, for a period of time I offered a free copy of my e-book, *Creating Your Personal Life Plan*,[1] to everyone who signed up to receive my blog updates via e-mail. In the first six months, I generated 23,326 subscriptions.

  Interweave Company does free extremely well. They have several online hobby communities, one of which is for quilters. Quilting Arts is the number one online community for contemporary quilters. If you join, there are five immediate freebies you can download, including patterns, project instructions, and more.[2]

- **Generate customer reviews.** A few years ago, Thomas Nelson launched BookSneeze,[3] a website designed to get its books into the hands of bloggers (sneezers) who could "infect" their readers. We let bloggers choose which books they wanted to review in exchange for an honest review on their blog. The program now has over twenty thousand bloggers participating in it. It has generated thousands of reviews for Thomas Nelson.

- **Provide product samples.** Assuming you have a great product—and this is a prerequisite!—the best thing you can do is seed the market with free samples. For example, awhile back, I gave away one hundred free copies of Marcus Buckingham's new book, *StandOut*. I generated 1,353 comments, 567 retweets, and 340 Facebook shares. More importantly for the publisher, it helped drive the book to number four on Amazon.com's overall sales ranking.

So how does this apply to you? Simple. You should use free to drive your marketing strategy. This can help you build your platform and launch your products. Here are ten quick idea starters to make free work for you.

1. **Offer free samples of your product to potential customers.** This could be the first two chapters of your book, the first two songs from your album, a small sample of your product, a one-time consult for a service, or a recording of you performing live.
2. **Offer an e-book or special report in exchange for newsletter subscriptions.** HubSpot is a master at this. As I write this chapter, they're offering a free e-book download of *10 Commandments of Marketing Automation*.[4]
3. **Offer a free copy of your product to bloggers in exchange for an honest review on their blog.** Start with the bloggers you know and follow.
4. **Offer multiple free copies of your product to bigger bloggers.** In return, they'll talk about your product and organize a giveaway to their many subscribers. You can offer fewer copies for smaller blogs and more copies for larger ones.
5. **Offer your time for free to people who buy various quantities of your products.** As we discussed in an earlier chapter, Gary Vaynerchuk did this for his book *Crush It!* to drive the best-seller lists.[5]
6. **Offer a free copy of the product in another format to customers who buy in your main format.** For example, offer a free copy of the audio book to everyone who buys the print book.
7. **Offer a free ticket to anyone who gets two of his friends to buy a ticket.** You will make it up in terms of merchandise sales and additional visibility.

8. **Offer free bonuses (e.g., workbook, group discussion guide, video course) to anyone who buys your main product.** It would be easiest to do this as a free download.
9. **Offer a free membership in your paid forum or club to anyone who buys your main product.**
10. **Offer a free seminar or performance and then sell your products at the event.**

There are literally hundreds of other ways you can use free to drive your marketing strategy and create visibility and excitement for your products.

FORTY

Stop Losing Readers

If you want to grow your platform—and obviously you do or you wouldn't be reading this book—you can't afford to lose readers. So many bloggers get in their own way and lose the audience they have fought hard to win. Why? Because they violate some very simple rules.

If you are at risk for doing the same, here's the message I would like to send you.

Dear [insert your name],

I am a very loyal person. I have been married to the same woman for thirty-three years. Most of my close, personal friends have been friends for a decade or more. I have gone to the same church for twenty-eight years. Once I let you into my life, I almost never ask you to leave.

This wasn't an easy decision. Your RSS feed has been in my Google Reader for a long time. Months. Perhaps years. But I finally clicked on the unsubscribe button. I've had enough.

Why? It's likely for one of these six reasons:

1. **Your titles make me yawn**. Look, I am scanning a couple hundred blog posts and news items a day. If your title doesn't pull me into the content, what will? You need to spend as much time on the headline as you do the article. Don't be cute; tempt me.
2. **Your posts are boring**. I have tried to be interested. Really, I have.

But you don't use any stories, illustrations, or metaphors. Your prose is preachy and didactic. And dry as dust. You're making my eyes glaze over.

3. **Your posts are too infrequent**. You haven't posted in weeks. Or months. Like so many would-be bloggers, you started well, but you quit too early. I'm sure you have legitimate reasons, but I am tired of waiting. Nobody cares. Post or perish.
4. **Your posts are too long**. I know you want to do the topic justice. Prove your point. Consider every aspect. Answer the critics. And leave no stone unturned. But, honestly, you are wearing me out. If I want to read a book, I'll buy one. You're supposed to be writing a blog. A good rule of thumb? No more than five hundred words.
5. **Your posts are too unfocused**. One day you're blogging on this. The next day you're blogging on that. What is your blog about? Please remind me, because I am lost in the forest of your eclectic interests. You're not a Renaissance man (or woman). You are undisciplined.
6. **You don't participate in the conversation**. You either don't allow comments or don't participate in them. Your posts are hit-and-run. You come into the room, make your little speech, and leave the building. I'm sorry, but that is so last century. You're not that important.

Sincerely,
Michael Hyatt

FORTY-ONE

Watch These Metrics

When people are trying to get a feel for how meaningful your platform is, most look at specific social media stats as a proxy for this, including those specifically related to blogging, Facebook, and Twitter.

In order to get accurate blog stats, you should sign up for a free Google Analytics[1] account. This is the gold standard when it comes to reporting Web stats. It is relatively easy but different depending on the blogging system you are using and your configuration.

Here are six stats that most people fluent in social media deem relevant.

1. **Unique Visitors per Month**. This is the number of unique individuals who have visited your blog in the last thirty days. For example, one individual may visit your blog three times in one week, but this would only count as one unique visitor. Note: RSS and e-mail subscribers do not count toward your total. For a true count, you must add the number of subscribers you have to this monthly total.
2. **Page Views per Month**. This is the number of pages on your site that visitors have viewed in the last month. If you divide this number by your total unique visitors, you will get the average number of pages viewed by each visitor. This number is important to prospective advertisers on your blog. Why? Because they are basically buying the specific number of impressions their ad will get on your site.
3. **Percent Change in the Last Twelve Months**. This is the rate of growth in the last twelve months. Here's the formula: unique visitors in the last thirty days, minus your unique visitors for the same period twelve months ago,

divided by your unique visitors for the same period twelve months ago, multiplied by one hundred. For me, that would be 166,103 (unique visitors in May 2011), minus 54,326 (unique visitors in May 2010), divided by 54,326, multiplied by 100, equals 205.8 percent growth.

4. **Average Number of Comments per Post.** Not all commenting systems keep track of this stat. Disqus,[2] the system I use and highly recommend, provides an "analytics snapshot" that tells you how many comments you received today, last month, and all time. For example, last month I had 4,608 comments. Divide that by twenty posts, that is an average of 230 comments per post. This demonstrates how engaged your audience is with your content. You can also include the average number of Twitter retweets or Facebook shares or likes per post.
5. **Total Number of Blog Subscribers.** The people who subscribe via e-mail or RSS represent your most loyal readers or superfans. They have made the effort to sign up to receive your content. More importantly, they have given you permission to push content to them. This permission-based asset is arguably the most important one you have.
6. **Total Number of Twitter Followers or Facebook Fans.** These are the two primary vehicles you will use to get the word out about your new blog posts. While the total number of followers can be important, it is more important to show how engaged they are. How many times have you been retweeted in the last thirty days? How many Facebook likes or shares have you had? If you really want to get fancy, track your Klout score.[3] This is a measure of your influence with your audience.

Notice that I don't mention hits. Expunge this word from your social media vocabulary. The term *hits* refers to the total number of requests your blog or website makes to the server. For example, if you have a page with numerous images on it, some JavaScript programs, and excerpts from a dozen posts, you might have twenty to fifty hits per page load. This number is irrelevant—at least as far as traffic goes.

If you start tracking the stats mentioned above, however, I can almost guarantee you that you will start seeing growth. What gets measured usually starts improving.

FORTY-TWO

Embrace Twitter

One of the most important tools to expand the reach of your platform is Twitter. If you are not already tweeting (i.e., posting), I urge you to read this chapter carefully. Know that at one time I probably felt much of the same hesitation about it as you do.

What is Twitter? I'm so glad you asked. Twitter's home page says it best:

> Twitter is a real-time information network that connects you to the latest information about what you find interesting. Simply find the public streams you find most compelling and follow the conversations.[1]

Tweeting requires very little time. For starters, you can only enter 140 characters at a time. This means that you must post very short, to-the-point messages. In practice, this means that, as a Twitter user, you update several times a day, but it takes almost no time at all. I do most of it from my iPhone.

If you are wondering why in the world you should consider it, here are twelve reasons:

1. **It will enable you to experience social networking firsthand.** One of my pet peeves is people who pontificate on new technologies but have never actually used them. Real users can always tell the difference. There is no substitute for personal experience.

2. **It will make you a better writer.** Since Twitter only allows you to post 140 characters at a time, you are forced to be concise. In my opinion, this is one of the hallmarks of good writing. Short messages. Short paragraphs. Short sentences.

3. **It will help you stay connected to people you care about.** Twitter is one of the few technologies I've found that actually contributes to community building. In today's busy world, it's difficult to keep up with others. Twitter makes it easy—and fun. For example, I can stay connected to my daughter who is away at college or my friend Bob Goff, whom I only get to see in person a few times a year.

4. **It will help you see a new side of your friends.** In an odd sort of way, Twitter humanizes people and provides a context for better understanding them. If you follow me on Twitter, for example, you'll quickly see that I get excited, bored, frustrated, and confused—sometimes all in the same day. You'll also learn what is important to me and what drives me crazy.

5. **It will introduce you to new friends.** I have now met several new people via Twitter. These have contributed to my life in small but significant ways. My wife, Gail, and I have even had dinner with a couple we met via Twitter.

6. **It is faster than text messaging.** In a sense Twitter is a universal text messaging system. You can broadcast to all of your followers (i.e., people who subscribe to your Twitter feed) or send a direct message to just one. As a result, I have almost completely stopped text messaging. The only time I use it is to reply to someone who messages me outside of Twitter.

7. **It will make you think about your life.** As you answer the question, "What am I doing?" you start to see your life through the lens of the people following you. Interestingly, it has made me more intentional and thoughtful about my life.

8. **It will help you keep up with what people are talking about.** Via Twitter, I have learned about hot books, cool software, breaking news, and even

great restaurants. Because the information is coming from real people who care enough to tweet about it, I have found it more valuable and authentic.

9. **It can create traffic for your blog or website.** When I began tweeting, I noticed a 30 percent uptick in my blog traffic in thirty days. It may be related to the fact that I was in the news more or was writing more controversial posts. However, I also think it was related to the fact that I was tweeting every time I posted a new blog entry. This seemed to have a viral effect.
10. **It requires a very small investment.** Twitter itself is a free service. In terms of my time, I probably invest less than thirty minutes a day. Since tweets are limited to 140 characters or less, you can scan them in a second or two. Writing one usually takes less than thirty seconds.
11. **It can help build your personal brand.** When people hear your name, what comes to mind? What is your reputation? What is the "brand promise"? Brands are built incrementally, one interaction at a time. Twitter gives you one more way to build your brand, one tweet at a time.
12. **It is fun!** Twitter is just plain entertaining. Following your family and friends is kind of like watching reality TV. The difference is that you know the people and actually care about them. In this sense, it is even more fun, because you know more about the people from other contexts. Don't believe me? Give it a try.

There are probably some downsides to Twitter that I am either ignoring or not recognizing. But wouldn't you rather jump into the fray and shape the future of social networks rather than sit on the sidelines and throw stones? More importantly, Twitter has the power to completely reshape the way you do marketing—that is, reach your tribe and engage them.

But first you need to know the basics about Twitter.

FORTY-THREE

Understand Twitter Basics

So I've convinced you that you should give Twitter a look-see. This simple step-by-step guide will get you up and running fast. Just follow these eight steps.

1. **Set up your account.** Go to Twitter[1] to get started. Enter your name, e-mail, and password. Click **Sign up**.

   You will now be taken to a second screen where you can select a user name. This is the name by which you will be known on Twitter. What name should you use?

   Your real name is best—if it's available. If not, you can try using a middle initial or prefacing it with something like *the* or *real* (e.g., "TheFrankDavis" or "RealFrankDavis").

   Also, I recommend using initial caps and in-word caps. It will make your username more readable and memorable. For example, I use "MichaelHyatt" rather than "michaelhyatt."

   Now click on the **Create my account** button. That's it. You are now an official member of the Twitter community. Congratulations!

   Next, Twitter will assist you in getting started. It will explain what a tweet is and give you the opportunity to "follow" a few friends, popular people, or brands. You can opt out of these steps for now if you wish. Simply click the **Skip this step** link.

   Twitter will also give you a chance to see if some of your friends are on Twitter by checking your online address book. However, your contacts will have to be in one of the supported services: Gmail,

Hotmail, Yahoo, or AOL. Also, you'll only see users who have allowed their accounts to be found by e-mail address.

This wasn't that helpful to me when I initially started, since my contacts resided in Microsoft Outlook. I had a Gmail account, though, so I just exported my contacts from Outlook and then imported them into Gmail. It worked flawlessly. If you get stuck, forget this step. You can add your friends later.

2. **Tweak your settings**. Make sure you are on your Twitter home page. Click on the **Settings** link. You should be on the **Account** tab. Set the time zone.

   Do not check "Protect my updates" unless you only want those you approve to be able to get your updates. Frankly, if you check this, it will seriously limit the fun. Make whatever other changes you want. Click the **Save** button.

   Now click on the **Profile** tab. Upload your picture. This is important. Many Twitter users (including me) will not follow users without photos, because it is a telltale sign of a spammer. Remember that the maximum upload size of your photo is 700k, so you may have to resize your image to meet this requirement.

   Enter the rest of your information, including your location, website or blog (if any), and a brief bio. This, too, is important to keep you from being flagged as a possible spammer. Your bio can either be serious or fun, but it must be brief—no more than 160 characters.

   Note that you can also connect your Twitter account to Facebook on this page. This will post all your Tweets directly to Facebook. Personally, I don't recommend this, but you may want to do it. You can always change the setting later.

   When you are finished, click the **Save** button.

3. **Set up your phone**. Twitter is much more fun if you connect it to your cell phone. By doing so, you can receive updates from those you are following (or just some of them) as well as send your own updates. It's all done through text messaging (e.g., SMS). Be forewarned: while Twitter doesn't charge anything for this service, your phone carrier might. It's a good idea to check and make sure you are on an

unlimited text messaging plan. You don't want to be surprised with a big phone bill.

Again under the **Settings** link, click on the **Mobile** tab. Enter your mobile phone number and click on the **Start** button. Now take your cell phone and text message the code Twitter gives you to 40404 (the number will be different if you are outside the U.S.). Be patient. Eventually, Twitter will confirm that your device is registered.

If you are using an iPhone, Twitter is built into the operating system (at least if you are using iOS 5 and up). You can set it up by opening the **Preferences** app, scrolling down the screen, and touching the **Twitter** section. This will give you the ability to post updates to Twitter from within many iPhone applications, including the photo app.

While still on your cell phone, set up a contact named "Twitter." For the mobile phone number, use 40404. Now every time you want to send a Twitter update, you will send it to this contact name.

4. **Follow family and friends.** If you haven't done so already, add your family and friends by clicking in the **Search** field at the top of your home page. You can type in a username or first and last name. When you do, you will get a list of users who match your search criteria.

   You can also do a more advanced search (e.g., searching by location) by clicking on **Refine results** or by going directly to the **Advanced Search** page.

   You can begin following your friends by simply clicking on the **Follow** button. If you want to also follow them on your cell phone, then you can turn the **Device Updates** to **on**. Personally, I only follow my family and a few close friends on my cell phone. Regardless, you will be able to see everyone you follow on your Twitter home page.

5. **Learn the basic commands.** Think of Twitter as a room full of people, all sitting in a circle. It's a conversation. When you update your status, you are speaking to the whole group. Everyone can hear what you have to say.

   - *Replies*. If you want to direct your comments to one specific person in the circle, but loud enough that everyone else can hear, use the **Reply** function. You address the person by using his or her Twitter user name preceded by the @ symbol. For example:

@spencesmith I get my haircut at Dion's South in downtown Franklin.

Everyone who is following Spence and me will see the message, but I am specifically directing it to Spence. (Those who are not following *both of us* will not see the message in their Twitter feed.)

You can also use this protocol (@+user name) to refer to someone by name. That is, *mention* him or her. For example:

I'm headed to dinner at Tin Angel with @gailhyatt and @meghmiller. I am looking forward to trying the new menu.

The thing about mentioning someone using @ plus his or her Twitter name is these become live links. If someone who is following me clicks on one of the names, he will automatically go to that person's Twitter page. This will give him the opportunity to follow that person too.

- *Direct messages.* Continuing with the metaphor of a conversation with a room full of people, you can also use the direct message function. This is like whispering in one person's ear. He can hear you, but no one else can. You are directing the message to him and only him. For example:

  d lnobles Can you bring my Business Review notebook down to the cafeteria conference room?

  Or:

  d gailhyatt It looks like I will not be able to leave the office for another 30 minutes. Bummer.

  Twitter direct messages have largely replaced simple text messaging for me and many people I know.

- *Hashtags*. You are probably familiar with tagging photos with a short piece of text. Twitter has this capability too. The # symbol, called a hashtag, is used to mark keywords or topics in a tweet. It was created organically by Twitter users as a way to categorize messages. If you click on a hashtag, it will show you all the other tweets associated with that hashtag.

  I have attended many conferences at which an official hashtag was announced. This enabled everyone at the conference to track what others were saying about the conference.

  For example, someone might say:

  Man I loved @AndyStanley's opening talk. He never ceases to speak to me. #cat2011

  #Cat2011 was the hashtag for the Catalyst Conference in Atlanta in the fall of 2011.

- *Other commands*. You can add people you want to follow from your cell phone. Just type in "follow [username]." For example:

  Follow KenDavisLive

  You can check your stats—the number of people you are following plus the number of people following you—from your cell phone by typing "stats" without any additional text.

  To stop all Twitter updates to your phone, send:

  Off

  To turn them back on send:

  On

  You can find answers to almost every other Twitter question in the Twitter Help Center.[2]

6. **Start tweeting**. So now you are all set up. It's time to start tweeting. You can do this from your Twitter home page or from your cell phone.

   The main thing you need to know is that the message can be no longer than 140 characters. If you use the Web page, the entry field will automatically count your characters. After a while, you'll instinctively know how long this is. I rarely go over the limit. But if you do, it's no big deal. Your message will just be truncated.

   How often should you tweet? That's the thirty-character question. My daughter @meghmiller says, "Don't tweet more than six times a day." Personally, I think ten to twelve is the upper limit. Obviously, there's a balance here.

   The real issue is whether or not you are adding something of value. There's an old Jerry Seinfeld comedy routine called "Air Travel." In it, he talks about airline pilots who insist on telling us all about the route they are taking. (Like anyone cares.)

   He says, as passengers, we don't knock on the cockpit door and say, "Oh, by the way, I'm eating the peanuts now." (Obviously this was a pre-9/11 bit.) So why do pilots feel the need to update us? All we care about is getting to the destination.

   In like manner, no one probably wants to hear the blow-by-blow of your life—but some color commentary is good. However, this is definitely art, not science, so there are no hard, fast rules.

   Regardless, you should consider every Twitter update as a branding impression. You are developing a reputation with your online friends, so make sure you are adding something to the conversation.

   This is really no different than a face-to-face conversation. You want to say something that is interesting, helpful, or just plain entertaining. Don't overthink it, but don't just tweet the first thing that pops in your mind.

7. **Be careful**. You definitely need to be cautious. It's probably not a good idea to say something like, "I'm headed to the West Coast for a week. My poor, beautiful wife is going to be home all alone." Bad idea.

   I have also had some experience with stalkers, so you may only want to tweet *after* you have gone somewhere, not before. Otherwise, you might find people showing up to watch you. (Don't laugh. It has happened to me on several occasions.)

8. **Consider third-party apps**. An entire ecosystem has sprung up around Twitter. Here are some of my favorite applications:
    - *HootSuite.*[3] This is the application I use to manage Twitter on my desktop. It will even manage Facebook profiles and pages, LinkedIn, and several other social media services. It is great because it allows you to segment people by groups (or columns). I have groups for my family, close friends, colleagues, and so on. It is available for both desktop systems and mobile devices.
    - *Buffer.*[4] I use this application to schedule my tweets, so I don't flood my followers with a string of posts all at once. Instead, I put them in Buffer, and it spreads my tweets throughout the day. It gives you tremendous control. You can determine how often and at what times you tweet. It comes with extensions for the most popular browsers, so you can buffer a tweet directly from a Web page. It also allows you to buffer Facebook status updates.
    - *SocialOomph.*[5] I use this application to bulk-schedule a whole series of tweets. For example, I have identified my ninety most popular blog posts. I have written a tweet promoting each one. Via SocialOomph, I schedule one tweet per day at a specific time. I upload the text file to SocialOomph and forget about it. Everything is on autopilot. It will also post to Facebook. This is something you can't do with Buffer.

    It is easy to get overwhelmed with all the third-party Twitter apps. Don't. Start with HootSuite and then grow from there as you have the time and interest.

Twitter is best learned by using it. The most important thing you can do is get started. You really can't make that many mistakes—and the Twitter community is very welcoming and supportive. Just remember to have fun and enjoy the people you meet online.

FORTY-FOUR

Don't Write Off Twitter!

Recently, I did an interview with our local paper here in Nashville about my use of Twitter. The reporter asked me to respond to a few of the common objections people have to using Twitter. I came up with five. After the interview, I decided to crowdsource my followers on Twitter to see if I'd captured all of the objections. I tweeted this:

> *Please help with my research for a blog post: Why don't your friends Twitter? What are the reasons they give you?*

Surprisingly, I got five more objections for a total of ten.

I then created a poll in SurveyMonkey,[1] blogged about it, and asked my Twitter followers and blog readers to vote for the top three reasons their friends say they don't use Twitter. More than seven hundred people participated in the poll, and here are the results:

1. **"That just sounds silly."** This is precisely what I said to my friend Randy Elrod when he introduced the service to me. He wisely said, "You won't really understand Twitter until you try it." I still think that's right. Therefore, if you do not use Twitter, I challenge you to try it for two weeks. If you don't like it after two weeks, fine. At least you will know firsthand why it didn't work for you.
2. **"I don't understand how to do it."** I get this a lot. No problem. That is precisely why I wrote the last chapter, "Understand Twitter Basics." It assumes that some of you know nothing about Twitter, and it walks you through the basics. If you have non-Twitter friends, one of the

best things you can do for them when they are just starting out is help them with the material in that chapter. (You can refer them to my blog post,[2] if you'd like.)

3. **"I think it would take too much time."** At one point, I heard this objection so many times that I documented how much time I spent on Twitter a day. I wrote a blog post on it (of course). I will cover this in more detail in the next chapter. As it turns out for me, less than thirty minutes a day—if that.
4. **"It is too narcissistic or self-centered."** Twitter is one of those things that merely amplifies what you already are. If you are narcissistic, then Twitter will give you a way to become even more narcissistic. But you won't attract many followers. The key to that is being genuinely other-centered and generous. In fact, these qualities are precisely what get other people's attention and get rewarded on Twitter. To be successful with Twitter, it can't be about you. It must be about your followers.
5. **"I prefer Facebook or some other social media outlet."** Honestly, I am not a big fan of Facebook, but there is no point in arguing it. We're all different. Still, why choose? You can have both.
6. **"It is a poor substitute for real relationships."** That's what I thought at the beginning. I already have a rich social life. Why do I need superficial relationships? However, with the exception of one of my daughters, my entire family started tweeting at the same time. This allowed us to stay connected in ways we could never dream of before. Plus, I have met some fascinating people on Twitter who eventually became real friends and business associates.
7. **"I don't have anything interesting to say."** Don't sell yourself short. Your life is more interesting than you think. Why do you think reality television is so popular? People crave transparency and authenticity. They long to connect with real people living real lives. It gives them perspective and helps them see that their lives are normal.
8. **"I am concerned about my privacy."** I wrote the book on this—literally. In 2001, my book *Invasion of Privacy: How to Protect Yourself in the Digital Age* was published by Regnery.[3] Since that time, I have done

a one-eighty. For all practical purposes, privacy is dead. Via Google, people can find out more about you in ten minutes than was possible in a lifetime ten years ago. You might as well intelligently feed the Google search engines with what you want people to know about you. You need to be smart about it, but you are in control.

9. **"I don't see how it could help my business."** I know so many people now who have almost completely given up traditional marketing. They are doing most of their promotion on Twitter and seeing huge success. But unless you try it, you won't benefit from it.

   Minda Zetlin wrote an article on Inc.com called "Launch a New Product on Twitter," in which she reported on a company that discovered the power of connecting with its tribe:

   > Until last year, NAP, Inc.'s best known product line was its Sleepy Wrap baby carrier. But when the company launched the Boba Baby Carrier last year, it focused its efforts on social media, especially Twitter. "Prior to that, we were just using traditional online and print advertising," says Ashley Jewell, director of social media marketing for NAP. "We went from having one follower to selling out our whole inventory in a matter of weeks."

   NAP's experience shows what some marketing experts already know: Twitter is an incredibly powerful tool for creating buzz and an ideal way to get customers' attention for a new product, service, company, or location.[4]

10. **"I don't know how to get started."** Twitter is profoundly simple. You can sign up for an account and get started in sixty seconds. All you have to do is answer a simple question, "What are you doing?" in 140 characters or less. An even better question is this: "What has your attention right now?" You can post an update or two and start following your family or friends. The rest will take care of itself. Trust me on this.

There may be some valid reasons for objecting to the notion of Twitter—and *not* using it. But these ten objections aren't them.

FORTY-FIVE

Devote Thirty Minutes a Day

Twitter offers an unparalleled opportunity for brand building, social networking, and customer engagement.

But at what cost? you may be thinking.

Obviously, the service itself is free. I don't know how much longer the folks at Twitter can sustain this business model. Eventually, they will have to monetize it or the service will go away. But in the meantime, it costs you or your business nothing.

The learning curve itself is also inexpensive. You can get the hang of it in less than thirty minutes.

But what about the time it takes to tweet? Ah, yes, "the time."

This is the standard objection from people who haven't actually tried it. "How do you find the time to Twitter?" they ask. In my experience, it takes me less than thirty minutes a day.

Here's how the math works out. I am a fairly active Twitter user. I average about thirteen tweets a day. Most tweets take me fifteen to thirty seconds each. (Yes, I have timed them.) Don't forget, you only have 140 characters. It can't take much time. Nevertheless, let's be conservative and assume that it takes me thirty seconds for each tweet.

Thirteen times thirty is six and a half minutes. I probably spend another fifteen minutes a day scanning other people's tweets and responding to direct messages or replies. Even then, I am doing this during downtime—early in the morning as I am reading, in between meetings or projects during the day, or in the evening as a way of relaxing. Added up, that's just over twenty minutes a day.

In my opinion, that's not a big investment of time, especially for the benefits I receive. Think about what you can do in twenty minutes: check Facebook, take a power nap, play Angry Birds, sort and load the laundry into the washing machine, or make breakfast. These are all good things, some more valuable than others. My point is if you have time to do them, you have time to use Twitter. The key is to be intentional and not allow it to become a huge time suck.

FORTY-SIX

Get More Twitter Followers

I rarely meet a Twitter user who doesn't want more followers. A few argue that the numbers aren't important. They are only concerned with "quality followers." I'm not sure it is either/or, but I've noticed most of the people making this argument have very few followers.

Why would you want more followers? Three reasons:

- **More followers provide social authority.** Like any other ranking system, the higher your follower count, the more people assume you are an expert—or at least someone interesting. It may not be valid, but that's the way it works in a world in which there is a ranked list for everything.
- **More followers extend your influence.** Twitter is a great tool for spreading ideas. If you have ideas worth sharing, why wouldn't you want to spread them to as many people as possible? Twitter makes it ridiculously easy. The larger your follower count, the faster your ideas spread.
- **More followers lead to more sales.** You're likely on Twitter for one of three reasons: to be entertained, to network with others, or to sell your stuff. Whether it's a brand, a product, a service, or even a cause, more followers provide the opportunity to generate more leads and more conversions.

Before I tell you what I have learned about how to get more Twitter followers, let me tell you how *not* to do it.

Don't try to cheat the system. If something sounds too good to be true, it probably is. Unless you are a celebrity who has built a vast audience in some other media channel, attracting followers will take time and effort.

What about buying followers? (Yes, you can do this. Just Google it!) For starters, this is contrary to Twitter's rules.[1] Worse, followers obtained in this manner have no affinity for you. They are like sending direct mail to an untargeted, generic list. Worthless.

What about using special software that promises to increase your follower count? In the early days of Twitter, I used one of these programs. It did increase my follower count—dramatically. I thought I'd hit the jackpot. However, it didn't last.

These programs all rely on "aggressive following" and "follower churn"—which means you follow people solely in the hope they will follow you back. If they don't, you dump them and follow additional people.

My joy was short-lived. Twitter caught on and implemented a policy against this.[2] In fact, I know several people who had their Twitter accounts shut down for engaging in this behavior. It annoys other Twitter users and degrades the Twitter experience for everyone.

So instead of using illegitimate ways to build your follower count, I want to share with you twelve proven ways you can get more Twitter followers. With the exception of my brief experiment with aggressive following, this is how I have built my own follower count to more than 115,000 followers in the last three and a half years.

1. **Show your face.** Make sure you have uploaded a photo to your Twitter profile. I will not follow anyone without a photo. Why? Because the absence of a photo tells me that the user is either a spammer or a newbie. Use a good head shot, like I describe in chapter 15.
2. **Create an interesting bio.** Don't leave this blank. It is one of the first things potential followers review. Explain who you are and what you do. If you were a brand or a product (crass, I know), what would be your tagline? Include that in your bio. Also, be sure to include a city name. By the way, Twitter will not include you in search results unless you fill out your user name, full name, and bio.[3]

3. **Use a custom About page.** Your Twitter bio can only include 160 characters. It's not much room to tell your story or introduce people to all you offer. Consider creating a custom About page on your blog and linking to it from your short Twitter bio.[4] Then, when a prospective follower clicks on that link, he or she will find a page you have created just for Twitter users.
4. **Make your Twitter presence visible.** I can't tell you how often I have read an interesting post and wanted to tweet the link, but couldn't find the author's Twitter user name. So I gave up and moved on. Make it easy for people to follow you—and for others to promote you. Display links to your Twitter account in your e-mail signature, your blog or website, business cards—everywhere.
5. **Share valuable content.** This is probably my most important piece of advice. Point people to helpful resources. Be generous. Be inspiring. Use lots of links. Create content that other people look forward to getting and want to pass on to their own followers. This is the key to getting retweeted. (I think it's why, on average, I get mentioned in other people's tweets 173-plus times a day.[5])
6. **Post frequently, but don't flood your followers.** I do most of my blog reading early in the morning. I scan over 220 blogs and love to share the gems I find. I used to do this as I found them, which often meant a flood of eight to ten posts at a time. Now I use Buffer[6] to spread these throughout the day so I don't overwhelm my followers.
7. **Keep your posts short enough to retweet.** Retweets are the only way to get noticed by people who don't follow you. Therefore, you must make it easy for your followers to retweet you. Keep your tweets short enough for people to add the RT symbol and your username ("RT @MichaelHyatt"). For me, that takes up seventeen characters, including the space. This means my tweets can be no longer than 123 characters (140–17=123).
8. **Reply to others publicly.** I used to reply to people via direct message (DM), thinking my message was irrelevant to most of my followers. Because I wasn't replying in public, this made me look unsociable. So now I reply almost exclusively in public. The only people who see those messages are those who follow both me and the person I am

replying to—a small subset of my followers. So it's sociable but not annoying.

9. **Practice strategic following.** This is not the same as "aggressive following" (which I condemned earlier). By this I mean, follow people in your industry, people who use certain keywords in their bio, or even people who follow the people you follow. Some of these will follow you back. If they retweet you, it will introduce you to their followers. For example, I could use Twitter's advanced search feature[7] to find everyone within a fifty-mile radius of Nashville who has used the word *leadership* in his or her bio or a post.

10. **Be generous in linking and retweeting others.** Twitter fosters a culture of sharing.[8] The more you link to others, the more people will reciprocate. And that's precisely what must happen for you to grow your follower count. You need others to introduce you to their followers. But don't *ask* for a retweet;[9] simply post content worth retweeting.

11. **Avoid too much promotion.** Yes, you can promote your blog posts, products, events, and more on Twitter, but be careful. There's an invisible line you must not cross. If you do, you look like a spammer—or just clueless. Not only will you not get additional followers, you will wear out your existing followers and many of them will unfollow you. This is why I advocate the 20-to-1 rule (see chapter 56).

12. **Don't use an auto-responder.** I used to use SocialOomph[10] to thank everyone who followed me and provide a link to my blog post "Beginner's Guide to Twitter."[11] I thought I was being courteous and helpful. As it turns out, I was being annoying. This is just more clutter in people's Twitter in-box. Avoid it. (By the way, I do thank people when they subscribe to my blog. However, this is primarily to let them know they have successfully subscribed. You don't need this with Twitter.)

Finally, don't worry too much about the numbers. If you follow the advice I have given above, the numbers will take care of themselves. Like most things in life, slow and steady wins the race. Don't underestimate the power of incremental growth over time. I didn't build my following overnight and neither will you.

FORTY-SEVEN

Keep from Getting Unfollowed

It's been demonstrated that Twitter is a great tool for extending the influence of individuals and organizations—extending your reach. With Twitter, you can engage your tribe in real time, offering leadership and assistance in a way that would have been impossible just a few short years ago.

For all that, my tweeting has not been without its challenges. I have probably made just about every mistake a user could make. Assuming you want to grow your influence and increase your follower count (and I realize that not everyone does), here are seven mistakes to avoid. We've discussed most of these in detail elsewhere. This is a quick list of reminders.

1. **Using a Difficult-to-Remember User Name.** If people can't remember your user name or have to look it up, most won't bother. As a result, you'll be left out of the conversation. In addition, a real name communicates authenticity and accessibility. Don't hide behind a made-up name that is only meaningful to you. If you want to change your user name to something better, you can do this in the Twitter settings panel without setting up a new account or losing your existing followers.
2. **Posting More than 120 Characters.** A retweet, by definition, will carry the abbreviation RT plus your user name. In my case, that would be "RT @MichaelHyatt" plus a space—seventeen characters total. That means my messages cannot be longer than 123 characters without requiring people to edit them before they retweet. If you want to get retweeted, make it easy for your followers.

3. **Tweeting Too Little—or Too Much**. Admittedly, this is a judgment call. Like the story of the three bears, somewhere between too little and too much is "just right." It depends on your goals and your audience's expectations. If you are only tweeting a couple of times a day or less, it is too little to get on most people's radar. If you are tweeting too much, you become annoying, and they will eventually unfollow you. Be wise and develop a strategy and be intentional about the number of messages you post.

4. **Asking for More than You Give**. Obviously, spammers and most direct marketers fall into this category. They mistakenly see Twitter as just another form of "interruption marketing." However, here I am referring to legitimate Twitter users who use their account to converse. But they also post too many messages promoting their company, products, or services. You must think of the Twitter community as a "social bank account." You can make withdrawals, but only if you deposit more than you take out. I shoot for a 20-to-1 ratio. In other words, I want to post twenty or so helpful resources or bits of information for every post in which I ask for help solving a problem, supporting a cause, or touting one of my company's products, and so on.

5. **Posting when You Are Frustrated or Angry**. Twitter is so immediate it is easy to post something in a moment of frustration that you later regret.

   Actor Ashton Kutcher found this out the hard way when he heard Penn State's revered football coach, Joe Paterno, had been fired. He tweeted, "How do you fire Jo Pa? #insult #noclass as a hawkeye fan I find it in poor taste."[1] Many of his eight million–plus Twitter followers quickly let him know they were outraged about this Tweet, since Paterno was fired for not reporting a child molester to police.

   After finding out the whole story behind the scandal, Kutcher tweeted, "This is an insane story, I just heard paterno was fired, getting the rest of the story now." He later posted, "Fully recant previous tweet! . . . Didn't have full story #admitwhenyoumakemistakes."

   And finally: "As of immediately I will stop tweeting until I find a way to properly manage this feed. I feel awful about this error. Won't happen again."

So before you respond in anger to something, take a deep breath and be sure you have all the details.

The problem with all written communication—especially Twitter—is that it is difficult to communicate context or nuance in your messages. Negative emotions are better expressed in person if they must be expressed at all. If you tweet these messages, you risk offending the person it was intended for and turning off a large percentage of your followers. Is this really the brand impression you want to create?

6. **Not Creating a Good Profile Page.** Your profile page is the first thing potential followers check. It should look intentional and be consistent with the brand image you are trying to convey. At the very least, upload your photo. This humanizes you by putting a face with a name. In addition, take the time to fill out the bio field. People want to know something about the people they follow. I even link to a custom About page on my blog that acknowledges the reader got there via Twitter and goes into more depth for those who are interested.

7. **Failing to Engage in the Conversation.** Just as your blog should not be a monologue, Twitter is not intended to be a monologue either. In fact, the entire premise behind Web 2.0—of which Twitter is just one technology—is that people want to engage in a dialogue. This makes it more demanding than other forms of media. In other words, unless you are a celebrity, you can't just broadcast your message and walk away. But this is also what makes it more powerful. When you engage with your customers and constituents, you have the opportunity to learn from them and influence them. Admittedly, I don't respond to every mention (see chapter 43, "Understand Twitter Basics"), but I do respond to every direct message, unless it is clearly spam.

This checklist should enable you to avoid some of the common Twitter mistakes. So if you are going to make mistakes, at least you can make different ones!

FORTY-EIGHT

Use Twitter to Promote Your Product

Twitter can be a fantastic tool for promoting your product or service. But I see very, very few people doing this well. They post some random tweets with no singular call to action and then wonder why their return on investment of time and energy was so low.

Twitter can be a key marketing tool for driving sales and the best-seller lists. But this works best if you take Twitter into account early enough in the product design and marketing process. This way you can formulate short, pithy tweets and get them into the hands of your biggest fans before you launch.

Here are nine ways to ensure you get the full benefit of Twitter for your marketing campaign. For simplicity I'll refer to products, but understand this applies to anything you're promoting, including yourself, another person, a service, music, or a physical product.

1. **Make sure the product has a title short enough to tweet.** One-word titles are perfect (e.g., AppStore or Mashable). In fact, that's why I chose *Platform* as the title of this book. Short phrases can also work. Long titles make it tough.
2. **Use a hashtag so you can collect the buzz.** A hashtag is used to mark keyword or topics within tweets. This protocol developed organically by Twitter users to categorize messages. Messages with the same hashtag show up together in a Twitter search. If you click on a hashtag, you will see all other messages using it. It is best if you can use a word in the product name or a shortened form of it.

3. **Make sure the product's Twitter user name is relatively short.** Of course, you can't go around changing your name—or the name of a person or product you're promoting—but if it goes beyond twelve to thirteen characters, consider using the first initial or two plus the last name (e.g., @MWBuckingham). The goal is to allow as much room as possible for the actual tweet.
4. **Decide on a landing page.** Where do you want to direct your followers for more information? It could be a custom website for the product (e.g., VibramFiveFingers.com), a product page on your main website (e.g., the "Creating Your Personal Life Plan" page in my blog[1]), or at the product page on an e-tail site like Amazon.
5. **Use a URL shortener.** I use bit.ly, but I have mapped a custom domain to it, so I get the value of branding. Mine is mhyatt.us. This enables me to turn something like this, which is a link to *Heaven Is for Real*, a recent bestseller published by Thomas Nelson . . .

   http://www.amazon.com/Heaven-Real-Little-Astounding-Story/dp/0849946158/ref=sr_1_1?ie=UTF8&qid=1316621485&sr=8-1

   into this:

   http://mhyatt.us/qnplTs

   If you have the patience to type the first one, try it. Both links get you to the same place, but one is dramatically shorter.
6. **Determine how long your tweet can be.** Everything up to this point is essentially metadata. It is not going to get anyone to click on the link or retweet the message. For that, you need an actual tweet. But how long can it be? To figure this out, deduct the length of the title, author name, hashtag, and landing page from one hundred forty (the maximum length of a tweet).

   For example, let's say I was creating a tweet for Andy Andrews's book *The Final Summit*. I might have the following metadata. Note that I converted the title to a hashtag:

   - Title: #FinalSummit (12 characters)
   - Author: @AndyAndrews (12 characters)

- Landing page: http://mhyatt.us/i6wQmo (23 characters)

If you total this, plus add three characters for spaces, you get fifty. Now subtract this from one hundred forty. This gives you ninety characters for your actual message. But wait. You should also allow room for retweeting (e.g., RT @MichaelHyatt). In my case, that is an additional seventeen characters, including the space. This means my message can only be seventy-three characters.

This doesn't sound like much room—and it's not—but you can make it work. Stay with me.

7. **Identify a series of tweetable messages.** These could be features and benefits of your product, great endorsements of your service, quotes from your book, or an exciting headline. Try to come up with short, pithy statements that can be used as tweets. They should be insightful, provocative, or intriguing. And, in the case of Andy's book (the example above), they can't be more than 73 characters long.

   Here are some examples from *The Final Summit*:

   - A dazzling gem cannot be polished without great friction.
   - A beautiful flower cannot be created without fertilizer.
   - Do not squander time, for that is the stuff of which life is made.
   - The winds of adversity fill the sails of accomplishment.
   - Nothing shows a person's character more than his habits.

   Shoot for twenty to thirty of these for each book.

8. **Put each tweet together, using the actual message.** I do this in a plain text editor like TextEdit on Mac or NotePad on Windows. Now you can copy and paste these into Twitter or automate the whole process. You can also make these tweets available to your brand evangelists on a special promotional page you have created for your fans to help get the word out.

9. **Automate the delivery of your tweets.** Caution: don't flood your followers with these messages or they will start to think of you as a spammer. I would post no more than one tweet a day—two at the most. Refer to chapter 56, "Practice the 20-to-1 Rule," for the reason why.

Having said that, you can subscribe to a service like SocialOomph, load your entire text file, and then schedule your tweets to appear twenty-four hours apart at a specific time of day. (You can also use HootSuite, but the options are more limited.)

Here is an example of a promotional tweet for a new book that includes all the elements I have described:

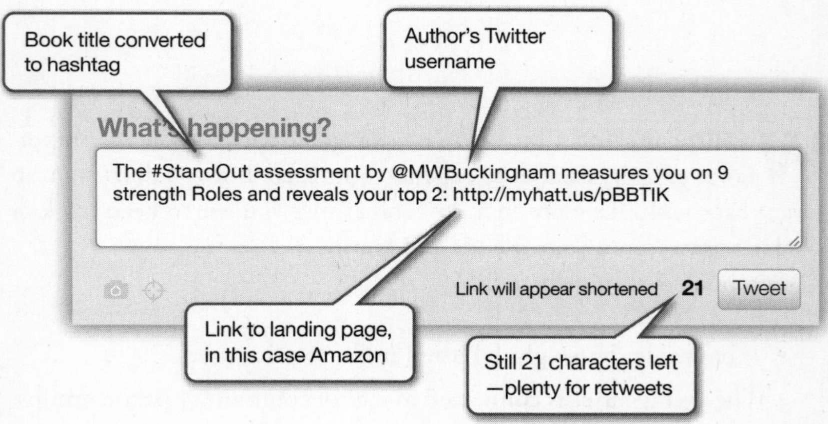

Yes, you can use Twitter as an integral part of your marketing campaign. The secret is to weave it in early—get preview tweets into the hands of your tribe to generate buzz—before either the product or the marketing plan is set in stone.

FORTY-NINE

Set Up a Facebook Fan Page

We've spent quite a bit of time—for good reason—on the importance of using Twitter to expand your reach. But you don't want to forget Facebook. It's more than just something you use to keep track of the latest news from your friends and family.

Facebook lists some incredible stats:[1]

- It has more than eight hundred million active users.
- The average user is connected to eighty community pages, groups, and events.
- On average, more than two hundred fifty million photos are uploaded per day.
- More than seventy languages are available on the site.
- More than 75 percent of users are outside of the United States.
- More than seven million apps and websites are integrated with Facebook.

Facebook's global reach is obvious, but still many people resist using it. I have vacillated on this myself. Then I came to the realization that Facebook itself is not the problem. I am. Facebook is simply a tool. It has its quirks and issues, to be sure. But the root problem was that I didn't have a strategy for how to use it.

Initially, my "friend policy" (if you could call it that) was to simply accept any and all comers. I figured the more friends, the better. But this resulted in a huge amount of noise, not to mention added workload. I grew weary of all the friend requests, invites, and notifications.

It also made me think long and hard about my vocabulary. Like many people, I had begun to use the term *friend* in a very loose way. The first thing I did in rethinking my strategy was to tighten up my definitions of key terms:

- **Family.** These are the people who are related to you by blood or by marriage. I have occasionally been too loose with this term. *Family* does not mean your close personal friends or your "work family." Calling them that is not accurate or helpful. It creates the illusion of something that is not true. It is best to use this word as it was intended.
- **Friends.** These are the people you know in real life. They are people you have met face-to-face, enjoy being around, and interact with in real life. (These three elements are key.)
- **Acquaintances.** These are people you have met online or off. You may know their names or even their faces. You may even have been friends at some point in the past, but you don't have an ongoing relationship. You only know one another on a superficial level, and that's fine. You just have to be clear that these are not your friends.
- **Fans.** These are the people who know your public persona or your work. This is also where you might get confused . . . because the relationship is not mutual. For example, I am a fan of Chris Brogan. We have even met once. I know lots of stuff about him, because of his blog and Twitter posts. This creates the illusion of intimacy. If I was not careful, however, I could fool myself into thinking I have a relationship with Chris. I don't. I'm just one of his many fans.

So with those definitions in mind, I set out to rethink my approach to Facebook. Basically, I have decided that I will only use my Facebook profile for family and close friends. This prevents my in-box from being flooded with sales pitches and invitations to things I don't care about.

Nonetheless, realizing that more people are on Facebook than Twitter and that at least 5 percent of my blog traffic comes from Facebook, I decided to create a fan page for everyone else who wants to connect with me.

For the record, I dislike the term *fan page.* It makes me very uncomfortable. Instead, I wish Facebook would use the term *public pages* for fan pages and *private pages* for profiles. I think that better represents the distinction between the two.

Regardless, my Twitter feed shows up in both places. The interaction on my fan page is more limited, though, which is what I need in order to preserve my sanity. My "fans" can write on my wall and I will reply back as I am able—just like I do with Twitter direct messages and replies.

Once I set up the fan page, Facebook tech support was kind enough to move all of my friends over to the fan page. I then proceeded to unfriend everyone on my profile page who wasn't a family member or a close, real-life friend. I went from over twenty-two hundred friends on Facebook to less than one hundred. It should be noted that the best way to do it now is set up your fan page and ask your Facebook friends to move to it. Some will. Some won't.

This was a slow and tedious process because I had to unfriend people one at a time. Facebook doesn't currently provide a way to unfriend people en masse. It took a few hours over several evenings to power through it. If I had to do it again, I probably would have just deleted my account and started over. It would have been easier.

Here are some of the key lessons I took away:

- You have to understand the difference between friends, acquaintances, and fans.
- If you try to be everyone's friend, you will be no one's friend. You must be deliberate and selective.
- You will probably offend some of the people you unfriended. That's okay. Your sanity and real friends are more important than meeting the expectations of fans and acquaintances.

- You need to be very careful whom you accept as a friend on your profile going forward. Just based on mouse clicks, it's three times as much work to unfriend someone as friend him.

In this crazy world of social media, I think we need to remain thoughtful and flexible about how we connect online, drawing clear distinctions between public and private. Nonetheless, what works today may not work tomorrow. What works with one hundred followers may not work with ten thousand followers. You should expect to rethink your online strategies at some point in the future.

FIFTY

Employ Consistent Branding

Let's assume that you are serious about starting a blog (a key to building your platform), so to support your blog and get your name out, you are going to develop pages on Twitter, Facebook, and YouTube. Are you content to upload your photo to all of them individually and be done with it? Or do you want a more consistent brand image, one that ties it all together?

Awhile back, I uploaded a new profile photo to Twitter. That didn't change my profile background, however, which still included my old headshot and a design done a few years ago by a professional designer. I decided to visit his page again and see what his company had to offer.

This particular designer specializes in templates and custom designs for Twitter, Facebook, and YouTube.[1] He provides his customers with the opportunity to create a consistent brand look across the three major social media platforms—and at an affordable price.

I elected to have him design all three profile pages. The cost? You might think it would have been in the thousands of dollars. But with this particular design firm, it was only a few hundred dollars. There are some good deals out there if you look for them.

Whether you design your own pages, or have them designed for you, here are four elements you want to include on a consistent basis across all platforms:

1. **Your Name.** Use it in exactly the same form in every instance. My friends may know me by either Michael or Mike, but in terms of my brand, I am only Michael.

2. **Your Logo**. It could also be a type font that is associated with your name. I use a "talk bubble" with an angled arrow at the bottom and a stylized "MH" reversed out of the box. This box is similar to the dialogue boxes you'd find in cartoons. The same idea was used on the cover of this book:

MH MICHAELHYATT
Intentional Leadership

3. **An Avatar**. Have your portrait done by a professional photographer, and use the same one in every application. Close-ups are best. If you are a public speaker, you may want to use an action shot.
4. **A Branding Statement**. This could be a slogan, a sell-line, or even the name of the product or service for which you are known—or would like to be known. I use the words *Intentional Leadership*, and I also incorporate a photo of a microphone, similar to the one on the cover of this book.

A consistent brand is vital for a strong platform. It's something I've worked hard to develop, and it should be one of your top priorities.

FIFTY-ONE

Be Prepared for Traditional Media

If you are successful with your online platform, you will inevitably be asked to appear on radio, television, or Internet shows to discuss your product, service, or cause. It's critical that you learn to do this well. Assuming you have a wow offering, nothing drives sales of it more than publicity.

I was thrown into the deep end of the pool with my first book. In the course of eighteen months, I did over twelve hundred interviews. I appeared on all three major television networks plus CNN, as well as national and local radio and television. During that time, I went through three rounds of professional media training. It was baptism by fire.

More recently, I have sat on the other side of the table, interviewing authors. I have hosted the Chick-fil-A Leadercast Backstage program for the last two years, during which I interviewed the speakers as they left the stage. In addition, I routinely interview authors for my own blog.

Sadly, while most businesspeople spend a lot of time perfecting their product or streamlining their service, very few hone their interviewing skills. As a result, their sales are not as successful as they should be.

Therefore, based on my experience as both an interviewee and an interviewer, I would like to offer ten tips for improving your interview skills:

1. **Prepare thoroughly for the interview.** Clearly, how you prepare will depend on what your business or cause is, but the advice is the same. Prep as if you're taking a college final, and have some materials with you that will help you remember important points. That way you won't have to worry about freezing up or suffering a mental block.

Remember Rick Perry's disastrous debate? He had an embarrassing brain freeze when trying to remember one of the three federal departments he advocated abolishing. Fortunately, you're allowed to have notes.

Many of my early interviews were about books I'd written. Before the publication of each book, I identified all the questions I might be asked. I then wrote three to four talking points in response to each question. I didn't write out the answer verbatim. Then I prepared a "briefing book," using a binder with one tab per chapter. Behind each chapter, I put the relevant talking points, statistics, and illustrations. I ad-libbed from that.

2. **Remember that the show is not about you.** It's not even really about your product or service. This is a big mistake many rookies make. You are not the star of the show. The host is. Or—perhaps more accurately—the audience is. Your job is to keep them interested in the topic, so they don't change the dial. This is key to the producer keeping his or her advertisers happy.
3. **Understand the audience.** You can't help the audience get what they want unless you understand them. Television shows, radio shows, and Internet shows are used to providing demographic and psychographic information to their advertisers. You can cut right to the chase by asking the producer or the booker for this information. In addition, before the interview begins it is a good idea to ask the producer if there is anything in particular you should know about the audience.
4. **Don't expect the interviewer to have done his homework.** Many first-timers complain that the interviewer didn't know a thing about what they had to offer. Trust me: this is the norm. Assume the interviewer hasn't prepped, and you won't be disappointed. And whatever you do, don't embarrass him on-air by asking! Instead, make the host look smart by providing the producer with a list of questions to ask. Nine times out of ten, you will be asked these exact questions. That has the bonus of making you look smart too!
5. **Be able to explain what you have to offer in a few sentences.** Many people cannot do this. They have never crafted an elevator pitch. You read

about that in a previous chapter, but here's the concept as it applies to the media: You get on the elevator of the NBC building in New York City. You suddenly discover that the producer for the *Today* show is standing next to you. Being polite, she asks what your newly invented widget does. You have ten floors to tell her—about fifteen seconds. What will you say? You need to write this out and memorize it. It should be no more than two to three sentences.

6. **Listen carefully to the questions.** It is easy to become anxious and interrupt the host. This is never a good thing—and you might find yourself answering the wrong question. Make sure you let the interviewer finish. Then affirm the question. Even if it is combative, you can say something like, "I totally understand where you are coming from. In fact, I had that same concern when I first started developing this product." Then answer the question—don't dodge it.
7. **Keep your answers brief and to the point.** There is nothing worse than a rambling guest who is missing the interviewer's cues. The host keeps trying to interject a point or "bring the plane in for a landing." Perhaps the producer has already cued the music, but the guest keeps right on talking. This is not good. A good interview is like a tennis match: The interviewer hits the ball over the net. Then the guest gets in position and hits it back, starting the cycle all over again. In addition, you need to speak in sound bites.
8. **Be energetic and authentic.** From the interviewer's perspective, there is nothing worse than a low-energy, superficial interview. If you are not excited about your offering, how do you expect anyone else to be? If you are doing a phone-in radio interview, stand up. Walk around. Smile. Even though your audience won't see any of this, they will hear it in your voice. Believe me, it makes a difference.
9. **Don't become defensive.** Don't expect the interviewer to throw you softballs. His or her job is to keep it interesting for the audience. You should expect tough questions and a little drama. This can actually help you win over the audience—if you have done your homework, and if you remain calm under fire. Resist the urge to become defensive. It only makes you look weak. Instead, agree where you can

agree. Follow the feel-felt-found formula: "I know how you *feel*. I *felt* the same way. But here's something I *found* in my research."

10. **Refer listeners back to your offering.** Publicity doesn't do you any good if you don't point people back at what you're trying to tell them about. If you're too aggressive, it will turn potential customers—and the host—off. If you are too laid-back, the publicity won't result in sales. Instead, mention your product or service, offer a few nuggets or free samples, and then refer people to your website for more information.

Creating your wow offering is half the job. The other half is embracing your role as the chief spokesperson. If you do this well, you have a chance of creating a long and successful career.

In fact, John Richardson, one of my blog readers, offered some suggestions on how to further improve your skills:

- **Join Toastmasters.** Joining a Toastmasters group will give you a place to practice your interviews before a live audience in a safe environment. Toastmasters has an entire speech manual for doing TV, radio, and other forms of live interaction.
- **Work with an image consultant.** If you are going to be on TV or video, how you look may be as important as what you say. Wearing the right clothes and having your hair professionally groomed can make a huge difference in your presentation.
- **Hire a voice coach.** If you are going to do radio, podcast, or live interviews, having the right vocal tone, pace, and inflection can really enhance the interaction. Learning how you sound and removing filler words such as *um*, *ah*, and *you know* will make you sound more professional.

John concluded with this observation: "While these three things may cost you a few hundred dollars, and some time, the resulting image and voice you portray to millions of people on TV will be substantially better and will ensure your desired goals are met."

PART FIVE

ENGAGE YOUR TRIBE

FIFTY-TWO

Get More Blog Comments

There's hardly anything more discouraging than blogging about something you think is important and then waiting for comments . . . and waiting . . . and waiting.

Conversely, there are few things more rewarding than having people comment on your post and engaging directly with your readers. More than any single factor, I think it is the one thing that has kept me blogging all these years. But how do you get more comments? How do you get your readers more engaged? Here are seven strategies I have found helpful:

1. **End your posts with a question.** The more open-ended you can make your posts, the better. I have found it helpful to simply end my posts with a question. Doing this is like sending your readers an invitation to participate. Pete Wilson uses this technique to great effect on his blog, *Without Wax*. Recently he posted "The Death of Gratitude,"[1] and ended with this question: "What's one thing you feel entitled to and are therefore missing the opportunity to be thankful for it?"

2. **Use a threaded comment system.** This allows your readers to comment in-line and reply to other readers. A great blog is not a monologue or a dialogue (allowing your readers to respond to you). Instead, it provides a mechanism for hosting a *conversation*, so your readers can respond to one another. On my blog I currently use Disqus[2] for this.

3. **Display your comment count prominently.** I can't explain this, but since I started displaying the comment count next to my post titles, the

number of my comments has increased dramatically. If the number is low, people want to jump in and be among the first to comment. If the comment count is high, readers think the topic is hot and want to get in on the action. Either way, you win.[3]

4. **Make it easy to comment.** Yes, comment spam is a problem. But most modern blog systems catch this without making it difficult for your readers to comment. (If you are using WordPress, you can simply install the Askimet plugin.[4]) If you are serious about this, don't insist on approving comments before they are posted live on your blog. Don't require registration and don't use some annoying technology like CAPTCHA[5] to prevent robot spam. It is no longer necessary.
5. **Participate in the conversation.** As we discussed in chapter 28, "Avoid Common Blogging Mistakes," if you start the conversation (your blog post), have the good manners to stick around and participate. Your readers want to engage with you. They will engage with other readers, but they are more likely to comment if they know you are reading the comments and replying to them. Yes, this takes time, but it is the best investment you can make if you want to get more comments.
6. **Reward your best commenters.** You can list your top commenters in your sidebar and recognize them publicly. You can do other kinds of giveaways or contests (though you need to be careful that you don't run afoul of the various lottery and sweepstakes laws). Be creative. People love getting something for free—or even at a discount.
7. **Don't overreact to criticism.** If people see you as sensitive, defensive, or rude, they will not feel free to participate in the conversation. This is true in real life; it is true on your blog. If you let people openly disagree with you, it adds to your credibility and encourages more engagement. The only time I delete comments—and it is very rare—is when they become snarky, offensive, or off-topic. (See chapter 55, "Develop a Comments Policy.")

There are many other ways to encourage comments, but these are some that have helped me. In the next chapter we'll talk about being selective about which comments to respond to.

FIFTY-THREE

Don't Respond to Every Comment

Comments are one major way in which blogging is different from all other forms of writing. You get near-instant feedback. This is tremendously gratifying, but it can also be a challenge to keep up with your readers.

During a recent six-month period, I saw my average number of comments per post double. The ensuing problem is this: even though I'd like to respond to every comment, it's simply not possible.

Think about it. If your blog audience grows to the point where you get fifty-plus comments per post, can you really reply to all of them? I doubt it—at least not consistently.

The good news is you don't have to. I don't, and I don't feel the least bit guilty about it. Here's why:

- **A blog conversation is like a dinner party.** You have invited everyone to your home for some food and conversation. Your content is like the appetizers. You offer it up to get things rolling.
- **The main course is the conversation itself.** Sure, the food is important, but the difference between a good dinner party and a great one is not the food. It's the interaction between the other people at the table.
- **As the host, you don't have to respond to every comment.** In fact, at a real dinner party, it would seem downright weird. It would draw too much attention to you. Instead, the party has to be about them—your guests.

- **You should be present and add value as appropriate.** I comment occasionally just to let people know I haven't invited them over and then disappeared. I also comment when I think I can add value by answering a question, clarifying something I said, or pointing my guests to additional resources.

The bottom line is you don't need to respond to every comment. Though this isn't scientific, I tend to respond to about 20 percent of them. You may want to do more or less. For me—for right now—this seems about right.

FIFTY-FOUR

Keep the Conversations Civil

If the current political climate in the U.S. is any indication, the lack of civility in public discourse has sunk to a new level. No one seems to listen to his or her opponents. Pundits (and politicians) routinely talk over one another. Volume appears to be more important than logic.

You might not be able to solve this cultural problem, but you don't have to put up with it on your blog. Recently, a representative of Publishers Lunch Deluxe commented on my blog post "Why Do eBooks Cost So Much? (A Publisher's Perspective)."[1] After noting the high number of comments, the editor said, "What also stands out is the civility of the discussion—even from those who might disagree—and the general appreciation from those who comment for an explanation from an executive."

This isn't an accident. I have tried to cultivate this environment over time. Why? Because I believe in the value of healthy, civil debate. I love leading and participating in meaningful conversations. I readily admit that I don't have all the answers. I learn from the community and especially my commenters.

But how do you keep the conversation on your blog healthy and constructive? How do you make it safe for people to disagree without becoming disagreeable?

Here are five tips:

1. **Use an industrial-strength spam blocker.** I use Askimet.[2] It is owned by Automattic, the same people who created WordPress. It stops comment spam dead in its tracks. Even though I get more than one

hundred spam or porn comments a day, Askimet weeds them all out. Occasionally, it mistakenly flags a comment that is not spam, but I have yet to see it let anything through that is spam.

2. **Create an official comments policy.** I will share mine with you in the next chapter. You can't expect people to follow the rules if they don't know them. As you can see, I am very clear about what I allow and what I don't. I include a warning with a link in the Post a New Comment box. I say, "Please note: I reserve the right to delete comments that are snarky, offensive, or off-topic. If in doubt, read My Comments Policy." (See chapter 55, "Develop a Comments Policy.")
3. **Participate in the conversation.** This is the most important tip. It's your party; people expect you to participate. If you don't, your blog becomes like an abandoned house. Don't be surprised if thugs vandalize it and spray digital graffiti on your posts. Maintaining an active presence keeps the conversation civil.
4. **Make your own comments stand out.** I make my comments stand out by highlighting them in a different color. This is easy to do if you are using self-hosted WordPress.[3] This way, people can scan down through your comments and readily identify those that are yours. People are much more likely to comment—and do so civilly—if they know you are on the premises.
5. **Be consistent with enforcement.** I rarely delete a comment, but some are so off-topic or belligerent, I must. Likewise, some commenters have to be banned. They are simply "trolls" spoiling for a fight and some perverted sense of feeling important. I don't put up with it. Their comments are like graffiti. If you let them stand, you will only get more of them.

Good comments, even from people who disagree, add value to your blog. You want to encourage these if you are going to build a community, but you also must protect your community from those who would abuse it.

FIFTY-FIVE

Develop a Comments Policy

I blogged for several years without a comments policy. But after a round of nasty comments, I decided I needed something to establish the rules of engagement. Without ground rules, some conversations were turning into shouting matches that discouraged others from participating at all.

As a result, I crafted a formal comments policy. It covers all the basics and has served me well. You are welcome to copy or adapt this policy for your purposes. In fact, I've reproduced it here so you wouldn't have to reinvent the wheel.

My Comments Policy

As you know, Web 2.0 is all about the conversation. But without a few simple ground rules, that conversation can turn into a shouting match that discourages others from entering into the fray.

So here is my comments policy. By posting on my blog, you agree to the following:

1. **You may comment without registering**. You can log in via Disqus, OpenID, Twitter, Facebook—or not at all. It's up to you.
2. **You may post anonymously**. I don't recommend this, but you may do so if you wish. I may change this rule if it is abused.

3. **You may post follow-up questions**. If you have a question, chances are you are not alone. Others are likely thinking similarly. Therefore, I would rather receive your comments on my blog than via e-mail. It is a better use of my time to address everyone at once rather than answer several similar e-mails.

4. **You may disagree with me**. I welcome debate. However, I ask that if you disagree with me—or anyone else, for that matter—do so in a way that is respectful. In my opinion, there is way too much shouting in the public square to tolerate it here.

5. **I reserve the right to delete your comments**. This is my blog. I don't have an obligation to publish your comments. The First Amendment gives you the right to express your opinions on your blog, not mine.

   Specifically, I will delete your comments if you post something that is, in my sole opinion, (a) snarky; (b) off-topic; (c) libelous, defamatory, abusive, harassing, threatening, profane, pornographic, offensive, false, misleading, or which otherwise violates or encourages others to violate my sense of decorum and civility or any law, including intellectual property laws; or (d) "spam," i.e., an attempt to advertise, solicit, or otherwise promote goods and services. You may, however, post a link to your site or your most recent blog post.

6. **You retain ownership of your comments**. I do not own them and I expressly disclaim any and all liability that may result from them. By commenting on my site, you agree that you retain all ownership rights in what you post here and that you will relieve me from any and all liability that may result from those postings.

7. **You grant me a license to post your comments**. This license is worldwide, irrevocable, nonexclusive, and royalty free. You grant me the right to store, use, transmit, display, publish, reproduce,

and distribute your comments in any format, including but not limited to a blog, in a book, a video, or presentation.

In short, my goal is to host interesting conversations with caring, honest, and respectful people. I believe this simple comments policy will facilitate this.

FIFTY-SIX

Practice the 20-to-1 Rule

One important word about building your brand via your platform: this is not something you should see as an opportunity to blast your message out to thousands of followers—for free!—and sell them stuff.

A thousand times *no*! Twitter, Facebook, Google+, and other social networks are *relational* tools, not transactional ones. Contrary to what many think, social media rewards generosity, other-centeredness, and helpfulness.

These tools are vehicles that appeal to our deep, (I believe) God-given desire to connect with others. They work when there is trust. When they become just another form of spam (violating people's trust), they fail to be effective.

For example, one Sunday morning, Chris Brogan posted a video review of his then-new Eagle Creek Tarmac 22 carry-on bag.[1] I happened to be in the market for some new carry-on luggage, and Chris is someone whose opinion I respect—especially since I know he is an experienced road warrior. I immediately went to the Eagle Creek website, found a local retailer, and bought one that afternoon. (I love it, by the way, and am still using it. Word-of-mouth in action!)

Chris wasn't trying to sell me. He wasn't engaged in marketing—at least, not in a traditional sense. He was simply being helpful by sharing something that he believed was valuable. And because I trust Chris's opinion, I took his advice and bought the luggage he recommended. This is how social media marketing works. You have to jettison the old interruption-based, traditional marketing model. It just doesn't work anymore.

But Chris wasn't asking me for anything. In fact, he rarely asks for a commitment from his followers or blog readers. Instead, he faithfully *gives* to his audience, day after day. He practices digital generosity. As a result, when he does ask for something, his followers and fans respond.

This phenomenon is what I have come to call the 20-to-1 rule. It represents a ratio. It means that you have to make twenty relational deposits for every marketing withdrawal. This isn't science. I don't have any hard, empirical evidence to prove it.

But I have observed that if you just keep asking people to do something—buy your book, come to your conference, sign up for your cause—without making adequate deposits, they will begin ignoring you. Eventually they will unfollow you and disconnect from your updates.

The fact is, no one wants to be spammed. Not today. There are too many alternative sources of content. If you want to build a social media platform—one where people listen to you—then you have to be a giver, not a taker. This is why the 20-to-1 rule is a good rule of thumb.

FIFTY-SEVEN

Monitor Your Brand

Whether you like it or not, people are talking about you, your brand, or your organization online. Right now. Do you know what they are saying? Do you *like* what they are saying?

As we discussed earlier, one important component of a social media strategy is building an outpost (see chapter 17, "Understand the Model"). This is a sort of intelligence agency or listening station that allows you to monitor online conversations. Anytime someone says anything about my company—or me—online, I know within minutes.

For example, when I was still CEO of Thomas Nelson, one of our retail partners wrote a blog post complaining that a shipment he had received from us was damaged. He was frustrated because it included some special order items that he had promised to one of his customers. As a result, he was put in the awkward position of having to call the customer and explain why his item would not be delivered as promised.

Because of my online monitoring system, I was notified within an hour of his post going live.

I was then able to go to his blog and comment on his post. I apologized and promised to solve the problem as soon as our office opened. The salesman in charge of his account also contacted him and offered to overnight the damaged books.

This kind of interaction has four benefits: 1) it allows you to solve your customer's problem; 2) it gives you immediate market feedback about your service; 3) it demonstrates that you are listening and responsive; and 4) it provides you with an opportunity to address the customer's public concerns (in this case by responding to his blog post, but an e-mail, a phone call, or a personal visit also works). This last point is particularly important. What is said on the Internet stays on the Internet. If you don't enter into the conversation, then it makes you look arrogant, incompetent, or both.

Here are the specific actions that you, as an individual or organization, can take to monitor your brand online:

1. **Sign up for Google Alerts.**[1] It's fast and super easy. Best of all, it's free. Once you do so, you can enter the names of those you want to monitor. I suggest you start with the following:

   Your personal name and its variations; the names of your key executives; the name of your company or organization; the names of your more important brands, products, or services; and the names of your key competitors.

   Now decide how you want to be notified. You can choose either email or RSS feed.

2. **Use Twitter search.**[2] You can use this handy little tool to also monitor for the same names you used with Google Alerts. You can then save the search for reusing or bookmark the search results page in your browser. As an alternative, you can create a search column in HootSuite or TweetDeck.

3. **Engage in the conversation.** If someone says something positive, you may want to thank him. If someone says something negative, you definitely want to respond. Otherwise, his side of the conversation is the only one on the record. You can do this in the same media the comment was originally delivered.

4. **Solve the problem.** You will get some credit for listening. You will get even more credit for responding. But your job is not finished until you follow through and solve the person's problem. Granted, you won't be able to satisfy everyone. But you should try. And whatever you do, don't blame the customer for the problem!

Again, people are talking about you online. The only question is whether or not you will participate in the conversation.

FIFTY-EIGHT

Defend Your Brand

It takes years to build a brand. Unfortunately, there aren't many shortcuts. You build a brand—like a reputation—one impression at a time. Every encounter with a customer results in either a "deposit" or a "withdrawal" in your "brand account."

Twenty years ago, if a customer had a bad experience with your company, it didn't matter quite as much. Sure, he could tell his friends, and if enough people had bad experiences, they could tell their friends. Eventually, it would catch up with you. But it didn't happen overnight.

But obviously things are different today. Digital communication has changed everything. If a customer has a bad experience, he can e-mail his friends, tweet his followers, or blog about his experience. In the blink of an eye, one bad experience can cascade into thousands—and even millions—of impressions. Brands can be damaged in a few days. That's why it is so vital that you monitor your brand online.

Here's an example of things going wrong. David Alston tweeted about his wife's bad experience with U-Haul. He said, "My wife just went through a totally rude customer service experience with our local U-Haul rep. Downright rude. Do they want the business?"[1]

Within seconds, this message was broadcasted to the fifteen hundred–plus people who followed him on Twitter. Within an hour, two dozen others used Twitter to share their own negative experience with U-Haul. Thousands of negative impressions ensued. The conversation snowballed.

David then cancelled his reservation with U-Haul and booked a truck with Penske.[2] He tweeted about the excellent customer service they gave him. This, too, snowballed.

In the space of a few hours, U-Haul lost thousands of dollars in revenue and Penske likely picked up thousands more. This doesn't even factor in the long-term damage to U-Haul's brand. All because U-Haul didn't understand the raw power of today's consumer.

This kind of experience gets replicated on Twitter hundreds of times a day. It also happens in e-mail messages, blogs, chat rooms, and discussion forums.

I experienced this phenomenon firsthand when I had a bad customer experience recently. I tweeted about the incident and then blogged about it. I was amazed at how people piled on with one bad customer-service story after another.[3]

This got me thinking. If you are responsible for building or maintaining a brand—and this includes every CEO, business owner, marketer, publicist, and customer service representative—you need to know how to defend your brand online. The stakes have never been higher.

Here are seven suggestions for defending your brand in the digital age:

1. **Build an online presence**. The time to build an audience is *before* you need it. You need people for whom you add value, a small army of followers, if you will, who can help you when you need it. This is why every CEO, brand manager, and department leader should create a blog, maintain a Facebook page, and get active on Twitter. There's no less-expensive way to create brand equity than by using these simple tools.
2. **Monitor the conversation**. You must use online tools to monitor what is being said about your company and your brands. I use Google Alerts to monitor news and blogs. I use HootSuite's built-in search function to monitor Twitter. (See chapter 57, "Monitor Your Brand.") These tools enable you to engage in the art of digital listening.

   As a result, I know within minutes when someone mentions me, my company, or one of my brands. I know precisely what is being said, by whom, and how I can respond if I choose to do so. It's never been easier to eavesdrop on what your customers are saying. And it doesn't cost you a dime.

3. **Respond quickly to criticism.** Like the old ad says, "Speed kills." If you don't respond quickly, you lose control of the conversation. It takes on a life of its own. For example, David Alston blogged about his bad experience with U-Haul at least twice. Nonetheless, as I am writing this, no one from U-Haul has yet posted a comment in response to either of his posts.

   A friend of mine, Anne Jackson, had a bad experience with American Airlines. She tweeted about it as it happened on April 6, 2008. She then blogged about it a few days later under the title "American Airlines Is the Devil."[4] Some thirty-eight people commented on the post, many with their own American Airlines horror stories.

   Anne told me that she was getting about thirty-five hundred visitors a day to her blog at that time. Another one thousand or so people heard about her experience via Twitter. If American had been monitoring its brand online, it could have been the first to comment on her post. Instead, thousands of people read about her experience, and then they read comments on her blog from other customers who had had bad experiences with the airline.

   For the record, on May 29, 2008, American called Anne, apologized for the "mix-up" back in April, and gave her seventy-five hundred award miles. It's astounding that it took them almost two months to respond. How many people read about Anne's experience in the meantime?

   Fortunately, American now has a very active social media department. I have had several positive interactions with them. They have dramatically improved their customer service through this channel.

4. **Admit your mistakes.** Why is this so difficult? When you mess up, the only—and I mean *only*—acceptable response is to take full ownership. "Sir, I am so sorry that you have had this experience. There is no excuse. We made a terrible mistake, and we're going to make it right."

   If you catch yourself apologizing and then using the word *but*, stop dead in your tracks and back up. That little conjunction should be like a blinking red light, indicating that you are not taking ownership.

   Unfortunately, the use of *but* completely negates the apology.

To quote Dr. Phil, "You can either be right or you can be happy." You can go a long way toward fixing a problem by simply accepting responsibility rather than blaming the customer or some other factor.

If you are going to apologize—and you should—make it a full apology. Avoid the word *but* like the plague. Take the hit to your pride and own the problem. The customer is always right. Even when he or she isn't.

5. **Understand the lifetime value of the customer.** I first heard the concept in Carl Sewell's excellent book *Customers for Life*.[5] Sewell was a Cadillac dealer in Dallas, Texas. It didn't take him long to figure out that his customers were worth more than a single transaction. He calculated that every customer is potentially worth $332,000, if he returns every few years and buys a new car. (The book was written in 1990, so at today's inflation-adjusted prices, it's probably worth twice that.)

   Now consider American Airlines. The lifetime value of their business customers is, I'm sure, worth tens of thousands—perhaps hundreds of thousands—of dollars. Fortunately, my experiences with American have been mostly positive. But if I had a bad experience like Anne's, think of the implications.

   For the fun of it, let's do the math. When I was CEO of Thomas Nelson, in a typical year I spent more than $12,000 with American Airlines. Now let's assume that I travel about the same amount every year, over a forty-year career (from age twenty-five to sixty-five). Based on this, in simple math, unadjusted for inflation, my lifetime value to American Airlines is $480,000. That's a big number.

   But this only begins to scratch the surface. That's what I am worth to American—just me. But what about everyone else in my circle of influence? When I was at Thomas Nelson, we probably had two hundred–plus employees a year traveling on American flights. I also have those who follow me on Twitter (currently over a hundred thousand) or read my blog (currently over fifty thousand readers a day). The ripple effect is significant. Millions of dollars are at stake.

   But I am only using American as an example. Again, I want to emphasize that my experience with them has been excellent. All things being equal, they are my airline of choice. My point here is more personal: What is the lifetime value of *your* customers or constituents? Have you ever stopped to calculate it? Not only do you need to understand what is at stake, but so do your people. It is literally the future of your business and your brand.

6. **Empower your employees—or yourself—to solve problems.** As a customer, there is nothing worse than having a head-on collision with bureaucracy. We've all been there. "I'm sorry, ma'am, but I'll have to check with my supervisor." Or worse, "I'd like to help, but we have a policy against that."

   Tim Ferriss, author of the best seller *The 4-Hour Workweek*, tells his employees and contractors, "Keep the customers happy. If it is a problem that takes less than $100 to fix, use your judgment and fix the problem yourself. This is official written permission and a request to fix all problems that cost under $100 without contacting me."[6]

   I think that's a reasonable approach. In fact, I have raised the ceiling to $200. I also request that employees notify their supervisor after the fact, so if there is a systemic problem that led to the bad customer service, it can be addressed and fixed once and for all.

   Ferris went on to note, "It's amazing how someone's IQ seems to double as soon as you give them responsibility and indicate that you trust them."[7] It's amazing how fast you can turn a bad customer experience into a good one when you empower frontline employees to solve problems immediately, without delay. Nothing communicates to your customers that your company values them more than this.

   Note that I also suggest you empower yourself to solve problems. By that, I mean be willing to spend whatever time and/or money necessary (within reason) to rectify a problem. Sole proprietors are often hesitant to make things right, because they realize that any money they spend comes directly out of their pockets. Again, when the value of a customer is taken into consideration, the decision becomes a little easier to make.

7. **Exceed your customers' expectations.** Every customer problem is an opportunity to create a wow experience. But it's not enough to meet their expectations—you have to exceed them. Anything less is merely restitution. It just gets you back to even.

Recently, I was having some memory problems with my MacBook Pro. I took it to the Apple retail store. The "genius" (that's literally what they are called) fixed the memory problem quickly, which is what I expected. He then returned my computer to me and said, "Mr. Hyatt, I hope you don't mind, but while we were checking your computer, we noticed that the battery was not seating correctly, so we went ahead and replaced it with a brand-new one." Wow! Now that's customer service—and one of the reasons I keep buying Apple products!

One final thought: it's also a great idea to listen to the conversations about your competitors. For example, if Marriott had a Google Alert set up for "Sheraton," they could listen online for customers who get frustrated with their Sheraton experience enough to blog about it. When it happens, they could be the first to post a comment. It might look something like this:

> I'm sorry you had such a bad experience at the Sheraton. I can't speak for them, but I can tell you that Marriott has been ranked #1 in the world for customer service by both Expedia and Hotels.com. As an incentive to give us a try, I'd like to extend a 20% discount to you and your readers. When you make your reservations, simply give the operator the following promotional phrase: "Experience the Difference." You can also use this if you make your reservations online. We look forward to serving you.[8]

If you have invested your time and money to build your brand, it is also worth your time to employ these simple tools and tactics to defend your brand.

FIFTY-NINE

Don't Feed the Trolls

As you build your platform, you are going to attract critics. It is inevitable. In fact, if you aren't attracting critics, you should be wondering why. Criticism is normal.

Why? Because if you have something important to say, you may upset the status quo and make people uncomfortable. Finley Peter Dunne once said about journalists, "Our job is to afflict the comfortable and comfort the afflicted." As a blogger, that might even be part of your mission. Unfortunately, this almost always meets with resistance.

Let's be honest: criticism hurts. At least it does for me. I've been in the public spotlight since my first book, *The Millennium Bug*,[1] hit the *New York Times* bestsellers list more than thirteen years ago. Writing three more books, becoming CEO and then chairman of a large publishing company, and launching a very public blog hasn't helped make me any less of a target.

Theoretically, I know this is just the price I have to pay. But emotionally, it always knocks me off-kilter.

One of the things that has helped me in the past few years is to distinguish between three types of critics:

1. **True Friends.** Not all criticism is bad. Heaven forbid that we should turn a deaf ear to everyone who disagrees with us. "Faithful are the wounds of a friend."[2] Some people are in our lives to save us from ourselves. As a leader—and a blogger—the trick is to create an environment that is safe for dissension, so these people can speak up.

2. **Honest Critics.** Some people decide they disagree with you and go public. They aren't malicious. They aren't out to destroy you. They simply disagree with you. That's okay. We need to allow for a diversity of opinion. Besides, you might learn something from it. It enriches the conversation. You need to engage these people and refrain from making it personal. Not everyone has to agree with you.
3. **Unhealthy Trolls.** These people have an agenda. They are out to hurt you—or at least use you for their own ends. They want to lure you into a fight. They taunt and mock you. They are unreasonable. If you engage them, they will only distract you and deplete your resources.

   The best thing you can do is ignore them. As someone once said, "Resistance only makes them stronger." You will never satisfy them. Just keep doing what you know you are called to do. See chapter 54 for a more thorough discussion of how to deal with comments that are over the line of civility.

You must learn to distinguish between these three. I assume that everyone is a friend or an honest critic until he or she proves otherwise. I may be naive, but I would rather give people the benefit of the doubt than live a life of paranoia.

SIXTY

Monetize Your Blog

I didn't start blogging to make money from it. The thought never occurred to me. When someone suggested I start accepting advertising, I resisted. I thought somehow it would compromise my integrity.

Then I realized that all professionals charge for their work. In fact, this is what separates the professionals from the amateurs. For example: Musicians sell tickets. Artists sell paintings. Authors receive royalties. Speakers are paid fees.

If you want to blog as a hobby, fine. But art and money aren't enemies. In fact, in most cases the former isn't possible without the latter.

You really can monetize your art without selling your soul. I make several thousand dollars a month using a combination of these three methods:

1. **Sell advertising.** You can start small with any number of WordPress plugins (one major reason to use self-hosted WordPress). I started with WP125[1] and started selling small 125 x 125 pixel ads. It generated enough income to cover my hosting costs and provide a little "fun money."

   As I developed momentum, I created a full-blown advertising kit[2] for potential advertisers. I used Google Analytics to gather the key metrics and then, using SurveyMonkey, conducted a reader survey to collect demographic and psychographic information.

   When my traffic got to about forty thousand page views a month, I applied to the Beacon Ad Network.[3] It is an online service that manages your ad sales. You can charge whatever you want per ad, but they take a 30 percent commission. They specialize in the Christian marketplace. Their sister-company, BuySellAds.com,[4] handles the general market.

By the way, I have never used Google AdSense. I just don't like the way it looks. However, it may have changed since I last evaluated it. If you are interested, John Saddington at TentBlogger.com has a terrific set of posts about AdSense.[5]

2. **Promote affiliates.** Here again, I started small. I signed up as an Amazon Associate[6] and started using my affiliate code in my links to books and other products. (I disclose this at the bottom of each post.) I now consistently make six to seven hundred dollars a month from these links.

   Later, I graduated to other products. For example, I promote Brett Kelly's *Evernote Essentials: Second Edition*[7] whenever I write about Evernote. I do this with complete integrity, believing it is the single best place to start if you want to get up and running quickly.

   I am also an affiliate for various other products like Standard Theme,[8] Nozbe,[9] and ScribeSEO.[10] The key is to find products you actually use and you believe will be beneficial to your readers. My own rule is if I don't use it, I don't promote it.

   If there is a product you are crazy about—especially an information product—it is worth checking to see if the publisher or manufacturer has an affiliate program available. You might also check Amazon. They sell way more than books.

3. **Sell products.** A few years ago, I wrote an e-book called *Writing a Winning Non-Fiction Book Proposal*.[11] I decided to turn it into a PDF file and sell it on my blog. It has sold consistently, month after month. In fact, I have yet to see sales decline.

   Last year, I decided to write a fiction edition called *Writing a Winning Fiction Book Proposal*.[12] It only sells about 50 percent of what the nonfiction one does, but it was still well worth the effort. I also sell both books as a bundle.

   The best thing about selling products like these—especially digital ones—is that they work while you sleep. The whole system is turnkey. Customers buy the books, the system provides a download link, and then the money is deposited into your PayPal account.

These methods are just the direct methods you can use to monetize your blog. You can also use your blog to generate leads for speaking, coaching, or consulting services—something I also do.

The key to monetizing your art without selling your soul is to offer ads, products, and services that are congruent with your brand and will add value to your readers.

CONCLUSION

Take the First Step

Several years ago, at the invitation of my friend Robert Smith, Gail and I attended a Tony Robbins seminar in Dallas, Texas. Much of the weekend focused on overcoming fear.

One particularly meaningful moment was the "fire walk," which occurred on the very first night of the event. All evening Tony had been talking about fear and how it so often holds us back from accomplishing the really important things in life.

I agreed with him—at least in theory. I had witnessed it countless times in my own life and in the lives of my family, friends, and business colleagues. As he continued to talk, I took copious notes, nodding in agreement.

But then Tony announced that we were going to participate in an experience that would force us to face our fears and serve as a powerful metaphor for our lives. We were going to walk on fire. Barefoot!

What? I thought. I looked at Gail. She looked at me. Our eyes were wide with fear, our jaws dropping to our chests. I mouthed the words to her, "Oh. My. God."

But there was no backing out. We were committed. Before we had left for the seminar, Robert had made us promise that we would play full-out. We had agreed to do whatever Tony asked of us, no matter what.

After about an hour of instruction, Tony led the entire audience—about fifteen hundred of us—outside to the hotel parking lot. There his staff had created twelve lanes of scorching hot coals, each about twelve feet long. The coals were white hot and crimson red, with tongues of fire dancing in the darkness. As we lined up to take our turn walking across, we could feel the heat—more than one thousand degrees!

Sooner than I wanted, I was the next person in line. I don't remember much after stepping onto the coals. I kept my head up and kept walking.

I remember getting to the end of the lane, having my feet rinsed with cold water, and feeling exhilarated. I had done it! Gail and I embraced and jumped up and down.

True to Tony's word, this has become a powerful metaphor in our lives. We have used it time and time again, whenever facing anything challenging or seemingly impossible.

What does this have to do with building a platform? Everything.

Setting out to develop a platform can be overwhelming and scary. There is so much to learn.

- What if you make a mistake or look foolish?
- What if they don't like you?
- What if you fail?

Let me tell you a secret. Forget all of that. Just like fire walking, *the key is to start*. Once you take the first step everything else will take care of itself. You will make it across the hot coals of fear, doubt, and confusion and reach the other side.

Of course, it's your choice. You don't have to take this journey. You can shrink back, give up, and live with regrets about what might have been.

But you will be missing out on so much!

Here's the question I always ask when I face a daunting task: "What would accomplishing this make possible?" More specifically, what would having a platform like I have discussed in this book make possible for your business, your cause, or your campaign? What would it make possible *for you*?

All you have to do is take the first step. You'll figure out the rest.

APPENDIX A

Comply with the FTC Guidelines

I am not an attorney, so the following is not legal advice. I am just sharing with you some things I do on my blog in my layman's attempt to be compliant with federal regulations.

A few years ago, the U.S. Federal Trade Commission (FTC) issued new guidelines that require bloggers to "disclose material connections" for product or service endorsements.[1] In fact, according to the Public Relations Society of America (PRSA), "People who blog, tweet or use Facebook to post opinions about consumer products could be fined $11,000 for repeat violations of new federal disclosure rules."[2]

I don't know how serious the FTC will be in enforcing these guidelines in the future. I have read some reports that indicate they will be primarily focused on advertisers who attempt to influence bloggers without requiring them to disclose that they were either paid or received free goods or services.

In an attempt to decipher the new FTC Guidelines, the PRSA says,

> The FTC dubs them [bloggers] "endorsers" and makes endorsers liable, along with advertisers, for false or unsubstantiated claims or for failing to disclose material connections between the parties.[3]

What does this mean? It means that if you have a "material connection" with a third-party advertiser or sponsor, you must disclose it. Specifically,

> Bloggers who receive cash or in-kind payment (including free products or services for review) are deemed endorsers and so must disclose material connections they share with the seller of the product or service.[4]

So how do we do this practically? A website called Cmp.ly (as in "comply") makes it simple for advertisers and bloggers to comply with the FTC guidelines.[5] They have created a series of easy-to-use disclosures and codes that you can use in conjunction with your blog posts, tweets, and other social media interactions. They provide a standard list of six disclosures:

1. No Material Connection
2. Review Copy
3. Free Sample
4. Sponsored Post
5. Employee/Shareholder Relationship
6. Affiliate Marketing Links

They provide graphic "badges" that you can insert in conjunction with your posts. The FTC does not require this, and personally, I find them intrusive. I want to comply with the law, but I don't want an additional distraction or clutter.

Originally, I thought it would be less intrusive to just insert a note after, for example, every affiliate link. As you probably know, if you mention a book on your blog and use your Amazon affiliate code, then Amazon will pay you a small commission when someone clicks through and buys the product. This approach looked like this:

> For the last week or so, I have been reading *Team of Rivals* [affiliate link] by Doris Kearns Goodwin. It is a page-turning account of Abraham Lincoln's presidency and his political genius.

But after living with it for a while, I felt this was also cumbersome and intrusive—especially with numerous links within one post, as I often have.

Therefore, I decided to include one blanket disclosure at the bottom of every blog post. Rather than using a badge, I use a simple block of text. It's a smaller font (though still readable) and a slightly lighter color. This approach looks like this:

> These same character flaws afflict many leaders today. The best safeguard is self-awareness.
>
> **Question: Do you see any of these flaws in your own leadership? What can you do to correct them now—while you still have time?**
>
> Disclosure of Material Connection: Some of the links in the post above are "affiliate links." This means if you click on the link and purchase the item, I will receive an affiliate commission. Regardless, I only recommend products or services I use personally and believe will add value to my readers. I am disclosing this in accordance with the Federal Trade commission's **16 CFR, Part 255**: "Guides Concerning the Use of Endorsements and Testimonials in Advertising."

I currently have the following five disclosure templates. I am inserting at least one at the end of each post.

- **Disclosure 1: No Material Connection**. This is the standard disclosure I use when I don't have any embedded links or a relationship with any of the products or services I have mentioned:

  > Disclosure of Material Connection: I have not received any compensation for writing this post. I have no material connection to the brands, products, or services that I have mentioned. I am disclosing this in accordance with the Federal Trade Commission's 16 CFR, Part 255: "Guides Concerning the Use of Endorsements and Testimonials in Advertising."

- **Disclosure 2: Affiliate Links.** This is the disclosure I use when I include an embedded affiliate link from Amazon or some other provider:

    Disclosure of Material Connection: Some of the links in the post above are "affiliate links." This means if you click on the link and purchase the item, I will receive an affiliate commission. Regardless, I only recommend products or services I use personally and believe will add value to my readers. I am disclosing this in accordance with the Federal Trade Commission's 16 CFR, Part 255: "Guides Concerning the Use of Endorsements and Testimonials in Advertising."

- **Disclosure 3: Review or Sample Copy.** This is the disclosure I use when I am reviewing a book or other product I have received from someone in the hope that I will review it:

    Disclosure of Material Connection: I received one or more of the products or services mentioned above for free in the hope that I would mention it on my blog. Regardless, I only recommend products or services I use personally and believe will be good for my readers. I am disclosing this in accordance with the Federal Trade Commission's 16 CFR, Part 255: "Guides Concerning the Use of Endorsements and Testimonials in Advertising."

- **Disclosure 4: Sponsored Post.** This is the disclosure I use when someone pays me to write a post for a product, service, or conference. I turn down more of these posts than I accept, because I have to be genuinely excited about the product:

    Disclosure of Material Connection: This is a "sponsored post." The company who sponsored it compensated me via a cash payment, gift, or something else of value to write it. Regardless, I only recommend products or services I use personally and believe will be good for my readers. I am disclosing this in accordance with the Federal

> Trade Commission's 16 CFR, Part 255: "Guides Concerning the Use of Endorsements and Testimonials in Advertising."

- **Disclosure 5: Employee/Shareholder Relationship.** This is the disclosure I use when I am writing about a book that Thomas Nelson, where I served as CEO, has published.

> Disclosure of Material Connection: I am a former CEO of Thomas Nelson, the company that published this book. Regardless, I only recommend books that I have personally read and believe will be good for my readers. I am disclosing this in accordance with the Federal Trade Commission's 16 CFR, Part 255: "Guides Concerning the Use of Endorsements and Testimonials in Advertising."

Feel free to borrow this method or any of my disclosure copy.

If you are using WordPress, you can also automate this whole process by using a plugin called Add Post Footer.[6] Just put your default text in the plugin configuration page. I use Disclaimer 2 for my default. Then you can override this on a post-by-post basis, using a custom field. The plugin documentation explains how.

APPENDIX B

Post Ideas for Novelists

Occasionally, when I speak on the topic of social media, I get push-back from novelists. "Yes, a blog may be a great way for nonfiction authors to build a platform, but what about novelists? What can we write about?"

Good question. Here are thirteen post ideas to get you started—a baker's dozen:

1. **Excerpts from Your Novel.** This is probably the easiest. It has the added advantage of allowing us, your potential readers, to "sample the brew." Just write a paragraph to set up the excerpt. Oh, and be sure to link to your book, so we can buy it (duh).
2. **Backstory of Your Novel.** Tell us why you wrote your novel. How did you settle on this story? How did you come up with the main characters? Why did you choose the setting you did? What research did you have to do before you could start writing?
3. **A Behind-the-Scenes Look.** Give us a sense of what it is like to be a novelist. How did you feel when you finally landed an agent? What does a typical writing day look like for you? What's it like to see your book in print and hold a copy in your hand for the first time?
4. **Director's Notes.** This is the kind of thing you occasionally see with extended versions of movies. Explain why you chose to start with a particular scene. Talk about the scenes you had to delete—or those you had to add to improve the story. Don't underestimate the curiosity of your readers.

5. **Interview Yourself**. Authors often complain that professional reviewers haven't read their book or don't "get it." Fine. Who knows your novel better than you? No one. So interview yourself! Have fun with it. What questions do you wish you would be asked?
6. **Interview Your Characters.** Imagine your novel is a movie and you can interview the actors who played the main characters. What would you ask them? What would they say? Another idea: if your novel was made into a movie and you could select the cast, what famous actors would you have play the main roles?
7. **Interview Other Novelists.** Find other novelists in your genre and interview them. In fact, build a circle of novelists who are similar to you and grow your tribe together. Interview one another. Perhaps even do book giveaways.
8. **Interview Your Editor**. Publishing still has a mystique about it and people want a peek behind the curtain. I find that my readers love this. Ask your editor what it's like to work with novelists. (If you're brave, ask what it was like to work with you.) Get him or her to tell stories about working with the best and the worst!
9. **Interview Marketers.** This is another variation on the last idea. Talk to the marketing people who work for your publisher. What's it like to market fiction? How is it different from nonfiction? How is it like marketing a movie? What makes it fun? What makes it challenging?
10. **Advice for Other Writers.** What tips and hacks do you have to offer other aspiring novelists? What advice do you have on coming up with the right story, securing an agent, meeting a deadline, or reviewing a marketing plan? Just answer the question, "What do I wish I had known then that I know now?"
11. **Common Obstacles.** What are the challenges you face as a writer? What was it like to be rejected (as you undoubtedly were)? What kept you going when you wanted to quit? How do you deal with writer's block or getting a negative review? Being honest and transparent humanizes you and strengthens the bond with your readers.
12. **Emotional Challenges.** These could be an extension of the last idea, but

focus on emotions. Certainly the writing experience brings out the best and the worst in us. Do you ever feel inadequate? Stuck? Overwhelmed? Disappointed? How do you deal with these emotions as a writer? How do you keep them from derailing you?

13. **Lessons Learned**. If you have written a novel, you have done what millions aspire to but few ever accomplish. What have you learned along the way—about writing, about publishing, about marketing—about yourself? Tell us so we don't have to learn the hard way.

I'm sure I am just scratching the surface, but this should get you started.

Resources

Here I have compiled a list of some of the best resources for building your platform.

BOOKS

Garfinkel, David. *Advertising Headlines That Make You Rich: Create Winning Ads, Web Pages, Sales Letters and More* (New York: Morgan James Publishing, 2006).

Godin, Seth. *Tribes: We Need You to Lead Us* (New York: Portfolio, 2008).

Klauser, Henriette Anne. *Write It Down, Make It Happen: Knowing What You Want and Getting It* (New York: Fireside, 2000).

Port, Michael. *Book Yourself Solid: The Fastest, Easiest, and Most Reliable System for Getting More Clients than You Can Handle Even if You Hate Marketing and Selling* (Hoboken, NJ: John Wiley & Sons, 2011).

Pressfield, Steven. *Do the Work* (Hastings-on-Hudson, NY: The Domino Project, 2011).

Schwartz, David. *The Magic of Thinking Big* (New York: Prentice-Hall, 1959).

Stephenson, Sean. *Get Off Your "But": How to End Self-Sabotage and Stand Up for Yourself* (San Francisco: John Wiley & Sons, 2009).

BLOGS

CopyBlogger website: www.copyblogger.com/blog.

Jeff Goins Writer website: goinswriter.com.

ProBlogger website: www.problogger.net.

TentBlogger website: tentblogger.com.

SOFTWARE

Acorn, published by Flying Meat Software: flyingmeat.com/acorn.
Anti-Social: anti-social.cc.
BlogJet, published by Coding Robots: www.codingrobots.com/blogjet.
BoxShot 3D: www.boxshot3d.com.
Business Card Composer, published by BeLight Software: www.belightsoft.com/products/composer/overview.php.
Call Recorder for Skype: www.ecamm.com/mac/callrecorder.
Cold Turkey: getcoldturkey.com.
FeedBurner mail list management: feedburner.google.com.
MailChimp mail list management: mailchimp.com.
MarsEdit, published by Red Sweater: www.red-sweater.com/marsedit.
QuickTime Pro, published by Apple: www.apple.com/quicktime/ extending.

WEBSITES

Amazon Associates: affiliate-program.amazon.com.
BufferApp: bufferapp.com.
CardFaves: www.cardfaves.com.
Cmp.ly: cmp.ly.
Compete: compete.com.
DomainTools: www.domaintools.com.
Google Analytics: www.google.com/analytics.
HootSuite: hootsuite.com
iStockPhoto: michaelhyatt.com/recommends/istockphoto.
Klout: klout.com/home.
Marketing Grader: marketing.grader.com.
Ping-o-matic: pingomatic.com.
Scribd: www.scribd.com.
SimplyVideo: www.simplyvideo.com.
SocialOomph: michaelhyatt.com/recommends/socialoomph.
TweetPages: tweetpages.com.
Twitter: twitter.com.
Vimeo: vimeo.com.

WORDPRESS THEMES AND PLUGINS

Add Post Footer: wordpress.org/extend/plugins/add-post-footer.
All-in-One SEO Pack: semperfiwebdesign.com.

Askimet: wordpress.org/extend/plugins/akismet.
Attention Grabber: attentiongrabber.tommasoraspo.com.
Beacon Ad Network: beaconads.com.
BuySellAds: buysellads.com.
Disqus: disqus.com.
ElegantThemes: michaelhyatt.com/recommends/elegantthemes.
GigPress: gigpress.com.
NivoSlider: nivo.dev7studios.com.
Public Post Preview: wordpress.org/extend/plugins/public-post-preview.
Scribe: michaelhyatt.com/recommends/scribeseo.
Standard Theme: michaelhyatt.com/recommends/standardtheme.
VaultPress: vaultpress.com/?utm_source=plugin-uri&utm_medium=plugin-description&utm_campaign=1.0.
WooThemes: michaelhyatt.com/recommends/woothemes.
WordPress: wordpress.org.
WP125: wordpress.org/extend/plugins/wp125.

OTHER RESOURCES

David Garfinkel, "Fast, Effective Copy" sales website, michaelhyatt.com/recommends/fasteffectivecopy.
EAHelp.com Executive Assistants: www.eahelp.com.
The SCORRE Conference website: www.scorreconference.com.

Notes

CHAPTER 1

1. For some strange reason, this video seems to have been removed from Apple's corporate website. However, Joachim Selke has archived them on his personal blog at blog.joachim-selke.de/2010/11/steve-jobs-macworld-2007-keynote-in-high-quality (accessed January 10, 2012).

CHAPTER 2

1. "One for One Movement," TOMS corporate website, www.toms.com/our-movement (accessed January 10, 2012).
2. "Top 10 of 2011: Overheard from the Giving Side," TOMS corporate blog, December 22, 2011, www.toms.com/blog/content/top-10-2011-overheard-giving-side (accessed January 10, 2012).
3. David McCullough, *1776: The Illustrated Edition* (New York: Simon & Schuster, 2007).
4. Eugene O'Kelly, *Chasing Daylight: How My Forthcoming Death Transformed My Life* (New York: McGraw-Hill, 2007).
5. "Sandra's Story," University of Miami School of Medicine, Cochlear Implant Center, http://cochlearimplants.med.miami.edu/patients/success_stories/Sandra's%20Story.asp.

CHAPTER 3

1. Josh Wilding, "Spider-Man: Turn Off the Dark's Preview Night Was a Disaster!" ComicBookMovie.com (blog), November 29, 1010, www.comicbookmovie.com/fansites/joshw24/news/?a=25796 (accessed January 2, 2012).

2. David James Young, "Spider Man Musical Preview 'an Epic Flop,'" DigitalJournal.com (blog), November 29, 2010, www.digitaljournal.com/article/300858 (accessed January 2, 2012).
3. Wilding, "Preview Night Was a Disaster!"

CHAPTER 5

1. Proverbs 29:18 KJV.

CHAPTER 6

1. If you search for this example, you will no longer find it: some time ago, Yahoo partnered with Match.com to form a new cobranded site called "Match.com on Yahoo."
2. "Yahoo! Personals Tagline: The Dating Game," Igor (website), www.igorinternational.com/process/yahoo-tagline-brand-engagement.php (accessed January 2, 2012).
3. *Building the Perfect Beast: The Igor Naming Guide* (self-published PDF), May 23, 2011, http://www.igorinternational.com/process/igor-naming-guide.pdf (accessed January 2, 2012).
4. Please note that these guidelines are primarily for nonfiction books and blog posts. Coming up with fiction titles is a whole other thing, though it seems like the strategy is usually to create intrigue—for example, *The Girl Who Kicked the Hornet's Nest* or *What the Night Knows*.
5. David Garfinkel, *Advertising Headlines That Make You Rich: Create Winning Ads, Web Pages, Sales Letters and More* (New York: Morgan James Publishing, 2006).

CHAPTER 7

1. SurveyMonkey (data collection resource), www.surveymonkey.com (accessed January 19, 2012).

CHAPTER 8

1. Yolanda Allen, "'I'm Not Babysitting Your French Fries!'—Take Responsibility for Running Your Own Business," BetterNetworker.com (website), July 1, 2010, www.betternetworker.com/articles/view/personal-development/discipline/im-not-babysitting-your-french-fries-take-responsibility-for-running-your-own-busi (accessed January 2, 2012).

CHAPTER 9

1. David Schwartz, *The Magic of Thinking Big* (New York: Prentice-Hall, 1959).
2. Henriette Anne Klauser, *Write It Down, Make It Happen: Knowing What You Want and Getting It* (New York: Fireside, 2000).
3. Ibid., 29–30.

CHAPTER 10

1. Dave Ramsey, *The Total Money Makeover: A Proven Plan for Financial Fitness* (Nashville: Thomas Nelson, 2003), 121.
2. Steven Pressfield, *Do the Work* (Hastings-on-Hudson, NY: The Domino Project, 2011).

CHAPTER 11

1. David Cornish and Dianne Dukette, *The Essential 20: Twenty Components of an Excellent Health Care Team* (Pittsburgh: RoseDog Books, 2009), 72–73.
2. Aileen Pincus, "The Perfect (Elevator) Pitch," Businessweek.com (website), June 18, 2007, www.businessweek.com/careers/content/jun2007/ca20070618_134959.htm (accessed January 2, 2012).
3. Michael Port, *Book Yourself Solid: The Fastest, Easiest, and Most Reliable System for Getting More Clients than You Can Handle Even if You Hate Marketing and Selling* (Hoboken, NJ: John Wiley & Sons, 2011), 49–60.

CHAPTER 12

1. See the Leatherman Argentum Collection website, www.leatherman.com/argentum/collection (accessed February 22, 2012).
2. Acorn, published by Flying Meat Software, flyingmeat.com/acorn (accessed January 3, 2012).
3. Business Card Composer, published by BeLight Software, www.belightsoft.com/ products/composer/overview.php (accessed January 3, 2012).
4. CardFaves.com website, www.cardfaves.com (accessed January 3, 2012).
5. WooThemes website, www.woothemes.com (accessed January 3, 2012).
6. ElegantThemes website, michaelhyatt.com/recommends/elegantthemes (accessed January 3, 2012).
7. Standard Theme website, michaelhyatt.com/recommends/standardtheme (accessed January 3, 2012).

8. TweetPages website, michaelhyatt.com/recommends/tweetpages (accessed January 3, 2012).

CHAPTER 13

1. Sean Stephenson, *Get Off Your "But": How to End Self-Sabotage and Stand Up for Yourself* (San Francisco: John Wiley & Sons, 2009), 168f.
2. EAHelp.com Executive Assistants, www.eahelp.com (accessed January 3, 2012).

CHAPTER 14

1. Paul Resnikoff, "Artists Say Facebook Likes Are Three Times More Valuable than Email Signups," Digital Music News (website), December 15, 2011, www.digitalmusicnews.com/permalink/2011/111215facebook (accessed January 2, 2012).
2. See Christopher McDougall, *Born to Run: A Hidden Tribe, Superathletes, and the Greatest Race the World Has Never Seen* (New York: Alfred A. Knopf, 2009).
3. Michael Hyatt, *Creating Your Personal Life Plan* (self-published e-book, 2011). Get a free copy here: michaelhyatt.com/life-plan.

CHAPTER 15

1. See "Smile," *Wikipedia*, last modified, December 30, 2011, en.wikipedia.org/wiki/Smile#Duchenne_smiling (accessed January 2, 2012).

CHAPTER 16

1. Michael Hyatt, "Keynote Speaker," MichaelHyatt.com (blog), michaelhyatt.com/product/speaking (accessed January 2, 2012).
2. "About Bloomberg Media," BloombergMedia.com (website), www.bloombergmedia.com/about (January 2, 2012).
3. Sundome 4 catalog page, Coleman (website), www.coleman.com/coleman/colemancom/detail.asp?product_id=2000007827&categoryid=11030&brand=#.TxIH4BwUVYU (accessed January 14, 2012).
4. Ibid.
5. See BoxShot 3D website, www.boxshot3d.com (accessed January 2, 2012).
6. Vimeo website, vimeo.com (accessed January 2, 2012).
7. "Bio," Ken Davis (website), www.kendavis.com/booking-info/bio/ (accessed February 1, 2012).

8. "Introduction of Michael Hyatt," MichaelHyatt.com (blog), michaelhyatt.com/myresources/michael-hyatt-business-audience-intro.pdf (accessed January 2, 2012).
9. Scribd website, www.scribd.com (accessed January 2, 2012).
10. "Crush It!—The Experience," Crush It (website), crushitbook.com/crush-it-the-experience (accessed January 2, 2012).
11. "The Jolt Experience," Jolt Your Life (website), www.joltyourlife.com/experience (accessed January 2, 2012).
12. My friend John Richardson recently outlined several possibilities, including links to vendors. See John Richardson, "Create Custom Resources for Your Speaking Business," *Success Begins Today* (blog), August 11, 2011, successbeginstoday.org/wordpress/2011/08/create-custom-resources-for-your-speaking-business (accessed January 2, 2012).
13. Final Summit Media Kit, Andy Andrews (website), www.andyandrews.com/ms/the-final-summit (accessed January 2, 2012).
14. You can download the PDF version of Andy Andrews's media kit here: www.andyandrews.com/ms/the-final-summit/Andrews-The_Final_Summit-MediaKit.pdf (accessed February 22, 2012).
15. EntreLeadership website, www.entreleadership.com/home (accessed January 2, 2012).
16. Dov Seidman (website), dovseidman.com (accessed January 2, 2012).
17. See Life After College (website), www.lifeaftercollege.org/book (accessed January 2, 2012).

CHAPTER 17

1. Chris Brogan and Julien Smith, *Trust Agents: Using the Web to Build Influence, Improve Reputation, and Earn Trust* (New York: Wiley, 2010). See michaelhyatt.com/recommends/trustagents (accessed January 15, 2012).
2. Jon Dale, "Using a Social Media Framework to Grow Your Tribe," JonDale.com (blog), July 7, 2009, jondale.com/blog/2009/07/using-a-social-media-framework-to-grow-your-tribe.html (accessed January 2, 2012).
3. See Hootsuite.com website, hootsuite.com (accessed January 3, 2012).
4. See Google Alerts website, www.google.com/alerts (accessed January 3, 2012).

CHAPTER 19

1. See Seth Godin's blog, sethgodin.typepad.com; Chris Brogan's blog, www.chrisbrogan.com; and Tim Ferriss's blog, www.fourhourworkweek.com/blog (accessed February 22, 2012).
2. See Compete website, compete.com (accessed January 3, 2012).
3. Guy Kawasaki's Twitter profile, twitter.com/#!/guykawasaki (accessed January 3, 2012).
4. Chris Brogan's Twitter profile, twitter.com/#!/chrisbrogan (accessed January 3, 2012).
5. Tim Ferriss's Twitter profile, accessed January 3, 2012, twitter.com/#!/tferriss (accessed January 3, 2012).

CHAPTER 20

1. This version requires that you host the blog on your own server or on a server you lease. It sounds more complicated than it is. Still, I only recommend this once you are generating some traffic and want to go to the next level.
2. BlogJet software, published by Coding Robots, www.codingrobots.com/blogjet (accessed January 3, 2012).
3. MarsEdit, published by Red Sweater software, www.red-sweater.com/marsedit (accessed January 3, 2012).
4. TypePad blogging software, www.typepad.com (accessed January 3, 2012).
5. MailChimp (mail list management software), published by the Rocket Science Group, michaelhyatt.com/recommends/mailchimp (accessed January 3, 2012).
6. AWeber (mail list management software), published by AWeber Communications, www.aweber.com (accessed January 3, 2012).
7. FeedBlitz (mail list management software), www.feedblitz.com (accessed January 3, 2012).
8. FeedBurner (mail list management software), feedburner.google.com (accessed January 3, 2012).
9. Ping-o-matic website, pingomatic.com (accessed January 3, 2012).

CHAPTER 22

1. iStockPhoto website, michaelhyatt.com/recommends/istockphoto (accessed January 3, 2012).

CHAPTER 23

1. James Pilcher, "Telling the Family You Lost Your Job," *Man of the House* (blog), December 1, 2011, manofthehouse.com/money/career-advice/telling-family-lost-job (accessed January 2, 2012).
2. Erin Glover, "Opening Night 1937: 'Snow White and the Seven Dwarfs' Premieres at Carthay Circle Theater," *Disney Parks Blog* (blog), December 21, 2011, disneyparks.disney.go.com/blog/2011/12/opening-night-1937-snow-white-and-the-seven-dwarfs-premieres-at-carthay-circle-theatre (accessed January 16, 2012).
3. See Flickr website, www.flickr.com (accessed January 3, 2012).
4. See the Creative Commons website for more information, creativecommons.org/licenses (accessed January 3, 2012).

CHAPTER 24

1. "Let Me Sleep on It: Creative Problem Solving Enhanced by REM Sleep," *Science Daily* (blog), June 8, 2009, www.sciencedaily.com/releases/2009/06/090608182421.htm (accessed January 2, 2012).
2. Anti-Social software, anti-social.cc (accessed January 3, 2012).
3. Cold Turkey software, getcoldturkey.com (accessed January 3, 2012).
4. LifeScapes Music website, www.lifescapesmusic.com (accessed January 3, 2012).
5. I liked what Ken was doing so much I became his business partner. You can find out more at the SCORRE Conference website, www.scorreconference.com (accessed January 3, 2012).
6. ByWord software, bywordapp.com (accessed January 3, 2012).
7. MarsEdit, www.red-sweater.com/marsedit.
8. iStockPhoto, michaelhyatt.com/recommends/istockohoto.
9. Scribe software, published by Copyblogger media, michaelhyatt.com/recommends/scribeseo (accessed January 3, 2012).

CHAPTER 25

1. Michael Hyatt, "How to Use Google Reader to Keep Up with Your Favorite Blogs," MichaelHyatt.com (blog), November 8, 2010, michaelhyatt.com/how-to-use-google-reader-to-keep-up-with-your-favorite-blogs.html (accessed January 2, 2012).
2. Call Recorder for Skype software, published by Ecamm Network LLC, www.ecamm.com/mac/callrecorder (accessed January 3, 2012).

3. QuickTime Pro software, published by Apple, www.apple.com/quicktime/extending (accessed January 3, 2012).
4. Duarte Design website, www.duarte.com (accessed January 3, 2012).
5. Public Post Preview plugin for WordPress, wordpress.org/extend/plugins/public-post-preview (accessed January 3, 2012).

CHAPTER 27

1. Michael Hyatt, "My Permissions Policy," MichaelHyatt.com (blog), michaelhyatt.com/permissions (accessed January 3, 2012).
2. DomainTools website, accessed January 3, 2012, www.domaintools.com.

CHAPTER 28

1. There are notable exceptions to this rule. Tim Ferriss usually only posts once a week, and he has enormous traffic.
2. PostRank website, www.postrank.com (accessed January 3, 2012).
3. CopyBlogger website, www.copyblogger.com/blog (accessed January 3, 2012).
4. Brian Clark, "How to Write Magnetic Headlines," *CopyBlogger* (blog), www.copyblogger.com/magnetic-headlines (accessed January 2, 2012).

CHAPTER 29

1. Michael Hyatt, "About," MichaelHyatt.com (blog), michaelhyatt.com/about (accessed January 2, 2012).
2. Ree Drummond, "About," *The Pioneer Woman* (blog), thepioneerwoman.com/about (accessed January 2, 2012).
3. Kate McCulley, "About Kate," *Adventurous Kate's Solo Female Travel Blog* (blog), www.adventurouskate.com/about-this-blog/about-kate (accessed January 2, 2012).
4. Ibid.
5. See my blog for the most current version: Michael Hyatt, "About," MichaelHyatt.com (blog), michaelhyatt.com/about (accessed January 3, 2012).

CHAPTER 30

1. Michael Hyatt, "Keynote Speaker," MichaelHyatt.com (blog), michaelhyatt.com/product/speaking (accessed January 2, 2012).

2. Michael Hyatt, "Creating Your Personal Life Plan," MichaelHyatt.com (blog), michaelhyatt.com/life-plan (accessed January 2, 2012).
3. Michael Hyatt, "The Fastest Way to Get a Book Contract—Guaranteed," MichaelHyatt.com (blog), michaelhyatt.com/product/writing-a-winning-book-proposal (accessed January 2, 2012).
4. Ibid.
5. Garfinkel, *Advertising Headlines.*
6. David Garfinkel, "Fast, Effective Copy" sales website, michaelhyatt.com/recommends/fasteffectivecopy (accessed January 2, 2012).
7. BoxShot 3D, www.boxshot3d.com.

CHAPTER 31

1. "Keynote Speaker," michaelhyatt.com/product/speaking.
2. Ibid.
3. SlideShare presentation–sharing channel (website), www.slideshare.net (accessed January 29, 2012).
4. SimplyVideo website, www.simplyvideo.com (accessed January 3, 2012).
5. iStockPhoto, michaelhyatt.com/recommends/istockphoto.
6. NivoSlider website, nivo.dev7studios.com (accessed January 3, 2012).
7. GigPress plugin for WordPress, gigpress.com (accessed January 3, 2012).
8. Ken Davis website, promote.kendavis.com (accessed January 3, 2012).

CHAPTER 32

1. WeeMacd, "What's the Point of Blogging? (or Maybe Just This Blog?)," *Enquire Blog* (blog), April 16, 2007, www.enquire.org.uk/youngpeople/wordpress/?p=47 (accessed January 2, 2012).
2. As quoted in Rick Warren, *The Purpose Driven Church* (Grand Rapids: Zondervan, 1995), 99.

CHAPTER 33

1. Seth Godin, *Tribes: We Need You to Lead Us* (New York: Portfolio, 2008).
2. Donald Miller, *Blue Like Jazz: Nonreligious Thoughts on Christian Spirituality* (Nashville: Thomas Nelson, 2003).
3. Wine Library TV website, tv.winelibrary.com (accessed January 3, 2012).
4. Acts 20:35 KJV.

CHAPTER 34

1. Hubspot's Marketing Grader website, marketing.grader.com (accessed January 3, 2012).

CHAPTER 35

1. WordPress website, wordpress.org (accessed January 3, 2012).
2. Google Analytics website, www.google.com/analytics (accessed January 3, 2012).
3. WordPress Standard Theme website, michaelhyatt.com/recommends/standardtheme (accessed January 3, 2012).
4. Jim Estill, "Shorter Is Better," *CopyBlogger* (blog), www.copyblogger.com/shorter-is-better (accessed January 2, 2012).
5. Scribe (website), published by Copyblogger Media, michaelhyatt.com/recommends/scribeseo (accessed January 3, 2012).
6. Disqus website, disqus.com (accessed January 3, 2012).
7. Garfinkel, *Advertising Headlines.*
8. "All in One SEO Pack," WordPress Plugin Directory, wordpress.org/extend/plugins/all-in-one-seo-pack/ (accessed February 1, 2012).
9. Scribe, michaelhyatt.com/recommends/scribeseo.
10. Jeff Goins, "Seven Steps to Writing a Successful Guest Post," MichaelHyatt.com (blog post), May 27, 2011, michaelhyatt.com/seven-steps-to-writing-a-successful-guest-post.html (accessed January 18, 2012).
11. Michael Hyatt, "An Invitation to Write for My Blog," michaelhyatt.com/an-invitation-to-write-for-my-blog.html (accessed January 18, 2012).

CHAPTER 36

1. MailChimp, michaelhyatt.com/recommends/mailchimp.
2. AWeber, www.aweber.com.
3. CopyBlogger blog, www.copyblogger.com/blog (accessed January 3, 2012).
4. ProBlogger (website), www.problogger.net (accessed January 3, 2012).
5. Hugh MacLeod's gapingvoid (website), gapingvoid.com (accessed January 3, 2012).
6. "About gapingvoid," gapingvoid.com/about (accessed January 3, 2012).
7. Hyatt, *Creating Your Personal Life Plan.*

CHAPTER 37

1. Google Analytics (website), www.google.com/analytics (accessed January 3, 2012).
2. If you use self-hosted WordPress, as I do, you can modify the single.php template file. If you use a different platform, the process will be different. You may want to get technical help. It's a simple procedure, but you will need to know a little PHP to make it happen.
3. SocialOomph (website), michaelhyatt.com/recommends/socialoomph (accessed January 3, 2012).
4. WooThemes, www.woothemes.com/.

CHAPTER 38

1. *Jeff Goins Writer* (blog), goinswriter.com (accessed January 2, 2012).
2. Leo Babauta, *Zen Habits* (blog), zenhabits.net (accessed January 2, 2012).
3. Brian Clark, *CopyBlogger* (blog), www.copyblogger.com/blog (accessed January 2, 2012).
4. *Chris Brogan* (blog), chrisbrogan.com (accessed January 2, 2012).

CHAPTER 39

1. Hyatt, *Creating Your Personal Life Plan*.
2. Interweave Quilting (website), interweave.com/quilting (accessed January 3, 2012).
3. BookSneeze (website), booksneeze.com (accessed January 3, 2012).
4. "Free eBook: 10 Commandments of Marketing Automation," *HubSpot* (blog), www.hubspot.com/marketing-automation-commandments (accessed January 2, 2012).
5. Gary Vaynerchuk, "Crush It!—The Experience," Crush It Book (website), crushitbook.com/crush-it-the-experience (accessed January 2, 2012).

CHAPTER 41

1. Google Analytics (website), www.google.com/analytics (accessed January 3, 2012).
2. Disqus, disqus.com.
3. Klout (website), klout.com/home (accessed January 18, 2012).

CHAPTER 42

1. "Twitter Is the Best Way to Discover What's New in Your World," Twitter.com/about (accessed January 18, 2012).

CHAPTER 43

1. Twitter (website), twitter.com (accessed January 19, 2012).
2. Twitter Support (website), support.twitter.com (accessed January 19, 2012).
3. HootSuite, hootsuite.com.
4. Buffer (website), bufferapp.com (accessed January 19, 2012).
5. SocialOomph, www.socialoomph.com.

CHAPTER 44

1. SurveyMonkey, www.surveymonkey.com.
2. Michael Hyatt, "The Beginner's Guide to Twitter," MichaelHyatt.com (blog), michaelhyatt.com/the-beginners-guide-to-twitter.html (accessed January 29, 2012).
3. Michael Hyatt, *Invasion of Privacy: How to Protect Yourself in the Digital Age* (Washington, DC: Regnery, 2001).
4. Minda Zetlin, "Launch a New Product on Twitter," *Inc.*, June 21, 2010, www.inc.com/managing/articles/201006/twitter.html (accessed January 2, 2012).

CHAPTER 46

1. See "The Twitter Rules," Twitter.com (website), support.twitter.com/articles/18311-the-twitter-rules (accessed January 3, 2012).
2. Ibid.
3. "How to Promote Your Profile," Twitter.com (website), support.twitter.com/groups/31-twitter-basics/topics/108-finding-following-people/articles/20005336-how-to-promote-your-profile (accessed January 3, 2012).
4. For example, see Michael Hyatt, "About @MichaelHyatt," MichaelHyatt.com (blog), michaelhyatt.com/about/twitter (accessed January 3, 2012).
5. "Social Analytics," Topsy Labs (website), analytics.topsy.com/?q=RT%20%40michaelhyatt (accessed January 3, 2012).
6. Buffer, bufferapp.com.

7. Advanced Search Feature, Twitter.com (website), twitter.com/#!/search-advanced (accessed January 3, 2012).
8. See Michael Hyatt, "Social Media and the New Culture of Sharing," MichaelHyatt.com (blog), July 29, 2010, michaelhyatt.com/social-media-and-the-new-culture-of-sharing.html (accessed January 3, 2012).
9. See Michael Hyatt, "Why I Won't Retweet You," MichaelHyatt.com (blog), January 17, 2011, michaelhyatt.com/why-i-wont-retweet-you.html (accessed January 3, 2012).
10. SocialOomph, www.socialoomph.com.
11. See chapter 43, "Understand Twitter Basics."

CHAPTER 47

1. Christie D'Zurilla, "Ashton Kutcher's Paterno Tweet Sends Actor Running for PR Cover," *Los Angeles Times* blog, November 10, 2011, latimesblogs.latimes.com/gossip/2011/11/ashton-kutcher-paterno-tweet-aplusk-ashton-kutcher.html (accessed January 2, 2012).

CHAPTER 48

1. Michael Hyatt, "Creating Your Personal Life Plan" (landing page), MichaelHyatt.com (blog), michaelhyatt.com/life-plan (accessed January 29, 2012).

CHAPTER 49

1. "Statistics," Facebook website, www.facebook.com/press/info.php?statistics (accessed January 2, 2012).

CHAPTER 50

1. TweetPages, tweetpages.com.

CHAPTER 52

1. Pete Wilson, "The Death of Gratitude," *Without Wax* (blog), November 21, 2011, withoutwax.tv/2011/11/21/the-death-of-gratitude (accessed January 2, 2012).
2. Disqus, disqus.com.
3. Implementing this will be different, depending on the blogging software you use.

4. Askimet plugin for WordPress, wordpress.org/extend/plugins/akismet (accessed January 3, 2012).
5. "CAPTCHA," *Wikipedia*, en.wikipedia.org/wiki/CAPTCHA (accessed January 2, 2012).

CHAPTER 54

1. Michael Hyatt, "Why Do eBooks Cost So Much? (A Publisher's Perspective)," MichaelHyatt.com (blog), November 2, 2010, michaelhyatt.com/why-do-ebooks-cost-so-much.html (accessed January 20, 2012).
2. Askimet plugin for WordPress, wordpress.org/extend/plugins/akismet. Also see the Askimet website for additional information: akismet.com (accessed January 20, 2012).
3. "How to Highlight Author's Comments in WordPress," *wpbeginner* (blog), September 3, 2009, www.wpbeginner.com/wp-tutorials/how-to-highlight-authors-comments-in-wordpress (accessed January 2, 2012).

CHAPTER 56

1. Chris Brogan, "My New Carry-On- Eagle Creek Tarmac 22," *Chris Brogan* (blog), April 18, 2010, www.chrisbrogan.com/my-new-carry-on-eagle-creek-tarmac-22 (accessed January 2, 2012).

CHAPTER 57

1. Google Alerts, www.google.com/alerts.
2. Twitter's search page is twitter.com/#!/search-home. You may want to bookmark this in your browser for quick access.

CHAPTER 58

1. David Alston, Twitter (status update), August 26, 2008, twitter.com/#!/davidalston/statuses/899484486 (accessed January 2, 2012).
2. David Alston, Twitter (status update), August 26, 2008, twitter.com/#!/davidalston/statuses/899606077 (accessed January 2, 2012).
3. Michael Hyatt, "Customer Service and the Butterfly Effect," MichaelHyatt.com (blog), August 25, 2008, michaelhyatt.com/customer-service-and-the-butterfly-effect.html (accessed January 2, 2012).
4. Anne Jackson, "American Airlines Is the Devil," Flowerdust.net (blog),

April 6, 2008, www.flowerdust.net/2008/04/06/american-airlines-is-the-devil (blog discontinued).

5. Carl Sewell, *Customers for Life: How to Turn That Onetime Buyer into a Lifetime Customer* (New York: Pocket Books, 1990), michaelhyatt.com/recommends/customersforlife.
6. Tim Ferriss, *The 4-Hour Workweek: Escape 9–5, Live Anywhere, and Join the New Rich [Expanded and Updated]* (New York: Crown Archetype, 2009), 105, http://michaelhyatt.com/recommends/4hour.
7. Ibid.
8. Please note: this is a purely fictional example.

CHAPTER 59

1. Michael Hyatt, *The Millennium Bug: How to Survive the Coming Chaos* (Washington, DC: Regnery Publishing, 1998).
2. Proverbs 27:6 KJV.

CHAPTER 60

1. WP125, a WordPress plugin, wordpress.org/extend/plugins/wp125 (accessed January 3, 2012).
2. You can download a copy here: michaelhyatt.com/advertising. It will give you an idea of what you need to create if you are serious about pursuing this.
3. See Beacon Ad Network, beaconads.com (accessed January 3, 2012).
4. See BuySellAds.com, buysellads.com (accessed January 3, 2012).
5. John Saddington, "A Blogger's Guide to Earning More with Google Adsense," TentBlogger.com (blog), September 19, 2011, tentblogger.com/adsense (accessed January 2, 2012).
6. See Amazon Associates website, affiliate-program.amazon.com (accessed January 3, 2012).
7. Brett Kelly, *Evernote Essentials: The Definitive Getting Started Guide for Evernote* (self-published PDF book, 2011), michaelhyatt.com/recommends/evernoteessentials (accessed January 3, 2012).
8. See Standard Theme website, michaelhyatt.com/recommends/standardtheme (accessed January 3, 2012).
9. See Nozbe website, michaelhyatt.com/recommends/nozbe (accessed January 3, 2012).

10. See Scribe website, michaelhyatt.com/recommends/scribeseo (accessed January 3, 2012).
11. Michael Hyatt, *Writing a Winning Non-Fiction Book Proposal* (self-published PDF book, 2010), michaelhyatt.com/product/writing-a-winning-book-proposal.
12. Michael Hyatt, *Writing a Winning Fiction Book Proposal* (self-published PDF book, 2010), michaelhyatt.com/product/writing-a-winning-book-proposal.

APPENDIX A

1. Federal Trade Commission, "FTC Publishes Final Guides Governing Endorsements, Testimonials," October 5, 2009, www.ftc.gov/opa/2009/10/endortest.shtm (accessed January 2, 2012).
2. Greg Beaubien, "New FTC Rules Spotlight Mommy Bloggers, but Target Marketers," *Public Relations Tactics* (blog), December 14, 2009, www.prsa.org/SearchResults/view/8468/105/New_FTC_rules_spotlight_mommy_bloggers_but_target (accessed January 12, 2012).
3. Michael Cherenson, "The New FTC Guidelines: Cutting Through the Clutter," *PRSAY* (blog), October 9, 2009, prsay.prsa.org/index.php/2009/10/09/the-new-ftc-guidelines-cutting-through-the-clutter (accessed January 2, 2012).
4. Michael Cherenson, "PRSA Offers Clarity on the FTC's Updated Guidelines to Regulate Blogger," *Public Relations Tactics* (blog), April 11, 2009, www.prsa.org/Intelligence/Tactics/Articles/download/6C-110929/1003/PRSA_Offers_Clarity_on_the_FTC_s_Updated_Guideline (accessed January 2, 2012).
5. See Cmp.ly website, http://cmp.ly (accessed January 3, 2012).
6. See Add Post Footer WordPress plugin, wordpress.org/extend/plugins/add-post-footer (accessed January 3, 2012).

Acknowledgments

A book is never the solitary work of a lone writer. So many people have shaped who I am today and in a very real sense, they were my collaborators on this project. Though I am sure I will forget someone, I'd like to especially thank the following people:

- My wife, Gail, for being my best friend, business partner, and lover for thirty-three years. She is a constant source of encouragement to me, always believing the best and forgetting the worst.
- My five daughters and (so far) three sons-in-law for keeping me real. While they love me unconditionally, they don't let me get away with *anything*. I only wish they had a little greater appreciation for my poor attempts at humor.
- My dad and mom, who have always noticed and affirmed what is best about me and overlooked the rest. They are two of the most positive, joyful people I know. No son could ask for more.
- Kristen Parrish, editor-in-chief at Thomas Nelson, and my editor on this project. We first worked together when she came to the company as my temp assistant in 1998. She rescued this project when I was ready to throw in the towel and demonstrated remarkable patience as I struggled to finish.
- Jamie Chavez, my copy editor, who hates the word *amazing* and who insisted that all my nouns and pronouns agree in number. She added the final polish that this project needed to shine.

- Brian Scheer and Joy Groblebe, my managers, and Tricia Welte, my executive assistant. The three of them handle the business side of my life, freeing me up to do what I do best. I couldn't ask for a better team.
- Andrew Buckman, my web developer, who implements my crazy ideas and keeps my blog running in tip-top shape. If I can conceive it, Andrew can code it. He also has the guts to push back when I suggest a bad idea.
- My downtown neighbors, also known as the "Franklin Campus," who are a wellspring of love and support. Thanks to Steve and Karen Anderson, Matt Baugher, Les and Patsy Clairmont, Ian and Anne Cron, Ken and Diane Davis, Chris Elrod, David and Rhonda Kemp, Lindsey Nobles, Bill Puryear, Keely Scott, Robert Smith, and Spence and Krissy Smith.
- My coaches, Daniel Harkavy, Dan Meub, and Ilene Muething. You taught me, stretched me, and pulled out of me stuff I didn't even know was there! You have shaped my thinking more than you know.
- My Community Leaders at MichaelHyatt.com, who help moderate my blog comments. You, too, free me up to focus on where I add the most value. You have given selflessly to my readers and I will be forever grateful. Thanks to Michele Cushatt, Barry Hill Jr., Joe LaLonde, Rachel Lance, Jim Martin, Tim Peters, Jason Stambaugh, Jeremy Statton, John Tiller, and Justin Wise.

Finally, I'd like to thank Morten Lauridsen, Eric Whitacre, Arvo Pärt, and John Tavener for providing the soundtrack for my late-night musings and writing. Oh yeah, and also Bon Jovi and 2 Limited for waking me up in the morning!

About the Author

Michael Hyatt has worked in the book publishing industry for most of his career. He got his start while a student at Baylor University and has since worked in every aspect of book publishing. He has also served as a literary agent and an artist manager. Most recently, he was the CEO of Thomas Nelson Publishers from August 2005 to April 2011. He currently serves as its chairman.

He spends most of his time now writing and speaking. His blog is one of the most popular in the world, consistently ranked in the top three on the topics of leadership, productivity, and social media. He also speaks on these topics to corporations and churches, and at various conferences.

He and his wife, Gail, make their home outside of Nashville, Tennessee.

Index

Contact Michael

To get the latest *Platform* updates and resources, visit:

michaelhyatt.com/platform

Michael speaks frequently on the topic of platform building. He can deliver a keynote, half-day, or full-day version of this content, depending on your needs. If you are interested in finding out more, please visit his Speaking page at:

michaelhyatt.com/speaking

You can also connect with Michael here:

Blog: michaelhyatt.com

Twitter: twitter.com/michaelhyatt

Facebook: facebook.com/michaelhyatt

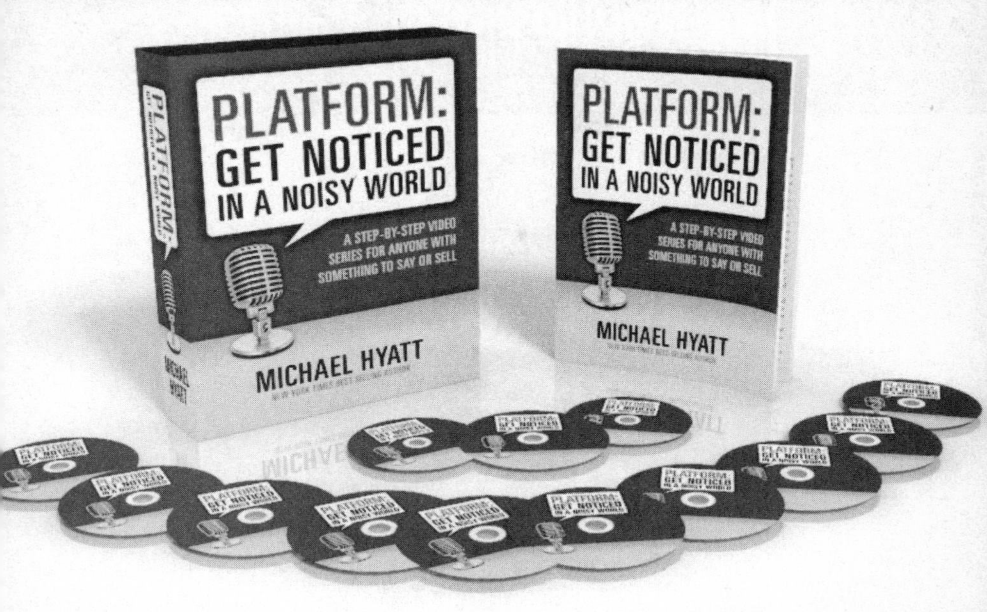

EXTEND YOUR REACH WITH THIS VIDEO SERIES BY MICHAEL HYATT.

Now that you've finished *Platform*, it's time to go deeper.

In this step-by-step tutorial, Michael will train you in the process of building a platform, sharing *exactly* what he did—and how you can do the same.

With the Platform Video Training, you'll learn everything you need to know to get your message heard in a noisy world.

ARE YOU READY TO MAKE YOUR VOICE COUNT?

GET STARTED NOW AT

MICHAELHYATT.COM/PLATFORMVIDEOTRAINING

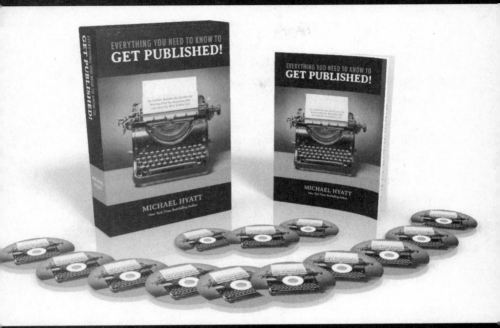